The Principal's Guide to a Powerful Library Media Program

The Principal's Guide to a Powerful Library Media Program

A *School Library for the 21st Century*

Second Edition

Marla W. McGhee
and Barbara A. Jansen

 LINWORTH

AN IMPRINT OF ABC-CLIO, LLC
Santa Barbara, California • Denver, Colorado • Oxford, England

Library of Congress Cataloging-in-Publication Data

McGhee, Marla W.
  The principal's guide to a powerful library media program : a school library for the 21st century / Marla W. McGhee and Barbara A. Jansen. — 2nd ed.
    p. cm.
  Includes bibliographical references and index.
  ISBN 978-1-58683-526-2 (acid-free paper) — ISBN 978-1-58683-527-9 (ebook)
  1. School libraries—United States—Administration.   2. Instructional materials centers—United States—Administration.   3. Media programs (Education)—Administration.   4. School librarian participation in curriculum planning—United States.   5. School libraries—United States—Evaluation.   6. Instructional materials centers—United States—Evaluation.   7. School principals—United States.   I. Jansen, Barbara A.   II. Title.
  Z675.S3M329   2010
  025.1'9780973—dc22   2010021243

ISBN: 978-1-58683-526-2
EISBN: 978-1-58683-527-9

14   13   12   11   10   1   2   3   4   5

This book is also available on the World Wide Web as an eBook.
Visit www.abc-clio.com for details.

Linworth
An Imprint of ABC-CLIO, LLC

ABC-CLIO, LLC
130 Cremona Drive, P.O. Box 1911
Santa Barbara, California 93116-1911

This book is printed on acid-free paper ∞

Manufactured in the United States of America

Copyright Acknowledgments

The author and publisher gratefully acknowledge permission to use excerpts from the following material:

Glickman, et al., *Supervision and Instructional Leadership,* © 2010. Reproduced by permission of Pearson Education, Inc.

Sergiovanni, *The Principalship,* © 2001. Reproduced by permission of Pearson Education, Inc.

Reprinted by permission of the Publisher. From Shirley M. Hord, *Learning Together. Leading Together: Changing Schools Through Professional Learning Communities.* New York: Teachers College Press. Copyright © 2003 by Teachers College Press, Columbia University. All rights reserved.

Children's Literacy Initiative, Philadelphia, PA, A Blueprint for Literacy Leadership was developed through funding from Wallace-Reader's Digest Funds.

Jean Van Deusen, *Teacher Librarian: The Journal for School Library Professionals K-12,* Vol. 23:1, p. 16–19, September/October 1995.

To my wonderful family, who always provides steadfast and unconditional love for me through all my endeavors, and to Mrs. Lorraine Burns, my favorite teacher, who even today continues to teach me new things.—M. M.

To my mother and friend, Marilyn Pinson, for her unconditional love and support, and to Bob Berkowitz, my good friend and mentor.—B. J.

Contents

Acknowledgments

A thank you from Marla ... Our collaboration began in 1989 when Barbara stepped into Live Oak as its new librarian. From that point on, learning on our campus was not the same. As a school community, we viewed the library program differently. We viewed collaboration differently. We viewed technology differently. Barbara joyfully and brilliantly worked side by side with teachers and students, facilitating deep thinking, creating meaningful research, and constantly promoting a love of literacy among all. I am so incredibly thankful for the years we worked together and I know I am a better educator today because of Barbara.

I want to extend a sincere thanks to my colleagues for their words of encouragement through this process. And, of course, a most heartfelt thanks to my lovely and supportive family—husband Tim, and daughters Sarah and Paige—for enduring many evenings at home without "Mom."

A thank you from Barbara ... Marla took a chance in hiring me, a first-year librarian, for her two-year-old school, Live Oak Elementary. She showed me that a supportive, collaborative principal provides the library media specialist with guidance when necessary but allows her the autonomy to develop a library media program that supports the intellectual needs of students and faculty. Under her leadership, I learned about best instructional practices and how to integrate them into the library media program. "How does this affect our students?" If the practice did not yield positive results and meaningful learning, then it did not become part of our methodology.

There are many others who have been instrumental in my growth as a professional: Mike Eisenberg and Bob Berkowitz, my Big6 colleagues, for their continued support and friendship, and for giving me opportunities to share effective strategies with others. Also helpful in the making of this book are my brave colleagues at Live Oak Elementary, Forest Creek Elementary, and St. Andrew's Episcopal School, who through the years have allowed me to collaborate with them to meaningfully integrate the information search process into their courses of study. Most importantly, to my husband, Larry, I owe a huge debt of gratitude for not complaining about being alone all those nights and weekends we worked on both editions of this manuscript.

From both of us ... There are many people who helped make this work possible. We would like to extend our sincere thanks to: Carlyn

Gray, Library Media Director in Round Rock Independent School District, for sharing many excellent library-related resources, some of which appear in this volume; Julie Walker, Executive Director of the American Association of School Librarians and our former colleague, for her energy and inspiration to always strive for something better; Carol Klahn, our long-time educational colleague and dear friend, for her incredible work as our indexer; and Mr. Bob Berkowitz and Dr. Carl Glickman for their powerfully written forewords that set the tone for this text. In this edition we owe thanks to the library media specialists and administrators with whom we have worked over the last five years, as many of the additions are a result of those collaborations.

About the Authors

Marla W. McGhee worked in the public schools of Texas for over two decades serving as a teacher, an elementary principal, a secondary principal, a curriculum area director, and a district-wide director of professional development. Under her leadership as principal, Live Oak Elementary was named a U.S. Department of Education Blue Ribbon School. In 1994 she was selected to represent Texas as the National Distinguished Principal, and was one of three finalists in the nation for the Principal in Residence position at the U.S. Department of Education in 1995.

Dr. McGhee teaches in the licensure and doctoral programs in Educational Leadership at Lewis & Clark College in Portland, Oregon. Prior to joining the Lewis & Clark faculty, she taught for nine years at Texas State University, where she was also the codirector of the National Center for School Improvement. In the 2008–2009 academic year, on leave from her university teaching post for one year, she returned to PK–12 public education to serve as Interim Director of Professional Development for the Austin Independent School District in Austin, Texas.

In addition to her work promoting the educational and instructional value of school librarians, library media centers, and information literacy, Marla's research and publishing interests include instructional leadership, action research as a school improvement tool, campus leadership for literacy learning, and the role of the contemporary assistant principal. Her works appear in such publications as *Phi Delta Kappan*, *Educational Administration Quarterly*, the *Journal of School Leadership*, and *Library Media Connection*. She holds two degrees in education from Texas Tech University and a PhD in Educational Administration from the University of Texas at Austin.

Barbara A. Jansen is the Chair of 1–12 Instructional Technology and Upper School Librarian at St. Andrew's Episcopal School in Austin, Texas. She is a consultant for the Big6 Associates. Before becoming a librarian, she taught at Berkman Elementary in Round Rock, Texas. Barbara specializes in integrating information process skills, content area curriculum, and technology. She has had articles published in *School Library Media Activities Monthly*, *Library Media Connection*, and *Multimedia Schools* magazines. Her books include the *Big6 in Middle Schools* (2007) and *The Big6 Goes Primary* (2009), available through Linworth Publishing. Barbara holds BS, MEd, and MLIS degrees from the University of Texas at Austin and is currently a student in the doctoral program in Information Studies. She is active in the Texas Library Association, where she serves on the Intellectual Freedom Committee. She is also a member of Texas Computer Education Association, American Library Association (ALA), American Association of School Librarians (AASL), and the International Society of Technology in Education (ISTE).

Barbara is committed to collaborating with teachers to fully integrate information and communications technology skills into the content-area curriculum. In 1994 she studied the Big6 model of information problem solving with Big6 co-authors Mike Eisenberg and Bob Berkowitz. They published a book titled *Teaching Information and Technology Skills: The Big6 in Elementary Schools,* also available through Linworth. Barbara is often asked to share her ideas at conferences and professional educational training seminars for state conferences, regional service centers, and local school districts and campuses.

Table of Figures

Contents of CD
(Selected Documents Available in the
Book and Appendixes)

CHAPTER 3: Quality Continuum of Instructional Time for Library Media Specialists

APPENDIX A: Administrator Self Assessments for Important Chapter Concepts
Administrator Self Assessment for Chapter 1
Administrator Self Assessment for Chapter 2
Administrator Self Assessment for Chapter 3
Administrator Self Assessment for Chapter 4
Administrator Self Assessment for Chapter 5

APPENDIX D: Library Media Specialist Interview Question Worksheet

APPENDIX E: Library Paraprofessional Interview Worksheet

APPENDIX F: Budget Proposal Worksheet

APPENDIX G: Blank Budget Form

APPENDIX H: Library Walk-About Checklist

APPENDIX I: Library Media Specialist Instructional Activities Feedback Form

APPENDIX J: Administrator's Library Media Program Feedback Form

APPENDIX K: Guide Sheets for Library Self Study
Library Media Program Budget Planning
Library Media Program Scheduling and Library Usage
Library Media Program Staffing Ideas

APPENDIX M: GEAR Worksheets for Concepts in Chapters 2 and 3, Including Blank Worksheet
GEAR Method Planning Guide for Concepts in Chapter 2
GEAR Method Planning Guide for Concepts in Chapter 3
GEAR Method Planning Guide Worksheet

Foreword

Robert E. Berkowitz, School Library Media Specialist
and Co-Creator of the Big6 Skills Approach

Those of us who are library media specialists understand the actual and potential impact of library media programs and library media specialists in the teaching-learning process. The problem is that it is not always the case that school administrators do.

This book takes the perspective that principals can make a significant difference in the quality of the library media program in their school through deep understanding and commitment to the importance of the library media program and effective partnership with the school library media specialist. It recognizes that principals can and must be partners in order to make school library media centers work.

The goal of this book is specifically and primarily to help school administrators lead their school community to high-quality use of the library media center for teaching and learning. To accomplish this goal, effective principals have to be instructional leaders who understand the importance of quality library media programs; administrators need the skills, ability, and information to:

- Facilitate the design, communication, and implementation, a vision for library media programs that is shared and supported by the school community
- Advocate, foster, and maintain a school climate and instructional program that supports the library media program

This book recognizes that the solution of under-utilized library media centers and under-appreciated library media specialists is deceptively simple. McGhee and Jansen present principles and perspective, and describe strategies that administrators can use to create a climate for successful library media programs. The topic strands addressed in this book: Philosophy, Curriculum Integration and Collaboration, Roles and Responsibilities, and Professional Development are essential vision elements. They provide perspective and direction to improve understanding and advocacy for school library media programs.

This guide can provide principals with a base of understanding about the characteristics of successful library media programs, and successful library media specialists, so that they can develop the capacity to support quality media programs. Principals must develop an understanding of and value for issues such as integrated information skills instruction, intellectual honesty and copyright, scheduling, program and staff evaluation in order to commit time, talent, and money to ensure that library media program goals are met.

This book should be a highly valuable resource for school principals, at any stage in their professional career, interested in improving their school's library media program. I trust that this text will be greeted with enthusiasm by principals as an important tool to help meet the challenge of creating, supporting, or maintaining successful school library media programs. Marla W. McGhee and Barbara A. Jansen have set out to help school leaders develop a shared sense of direction.

That's what this book is all about.

Foreword

Carl D. Glickman, President of the Institute for Schools,
Education, and Democracy and Professor Emeritus of
Education at The University of Georgia

While directing a school-university partnership, one campus I worked with for a number of years was a favorite place to visit. The school looked like a high-end wealthy facility with all the right roof angles, generous corridors, sunny classroom, and richly woven carpets. However, its students were not from wealthy homes—they lived in urban trailer parks and low-income housing projects. My pleasure in visiting was to experience the joy of watching these learners being so much a part of their school. They loved to read, to discuss books, and to ask incessant questions of how and why and when and what to each other and every one else who happened by.

After reading this text, I now understand why students and faculty were so drawn to reading, writing, researching, and exploring. A good part of the attraction was the library media center and an exuberant and skilled librarian. She and her aide and parent volunteers were physically located in the hub of the school, in open view of every person. The library was an inviting and attractive place for students to ask questions, listen to advice, find new information, use various forms of informative technology, and present and display their findings. The rapport between librarian, teachers, students, and parents was extraordinary. If you didn't know who was who, you could easily suspect that everyone and no one was in charge, as the hum of productive activity beckoned all into this place.

Marla McGhee and Barbara Jansen have done the profession a true service in writing this book, full of illustrations and real cases showing school principals how steady school improvement and higher student achievement comes about through integrative curriculum planning with teachers, administrators, and library staff; staff development conducted with and by staff; and open and purposeful flow of communication among library media specialists, teachers, students, and parents over classroom, curriculum, and student needs.

Perhaps many school leaders think, as I did as a school principal, that the library is an important place but best to be left alone in the hands of competent professionals. I now understand that the result of such benign neglect is terrible underutilization. The authors explain that the culprits are not the librarians or teachers, as in most schools they respect each other. But they simply don't have the time to make the library media center central to teaching and learning. It takes steadfast and knowledgeable leaders to change this detachment to powerful collaboration. This book will help school principals alter the role of the library media center to be a force for the public purpose of our schools—the advancement of engaged learning of *all students*—so critical to achieving the next generation of educated, resourceful citizens.

Introduction

The number of students enrolled in schools has never been larger, and the challenges facing students, educational professionals, school leaders, and parents have never been greater. Schools today are richly diverse places to learn—an amalgam of cultures and languages and an ideal forum for varied thoughts and opinions. Moreover, in a time when technologies are proliferating, communication is immediate, and communities are globally connected—managing, accessing, and making sense of information should be considered a standard or basic skill in a democratic society. Yet matters such as school funding, safety, campus overcrowding, and policies and pressures associated with increased performance and high impact testing are often shaping the way schools do business.

Considering these issues, there has never been a more appropriate time to enable campus professionals to do what they *can* do best. For the library media specialist this means spending time planning and teaching with classroom colleagues across all grade levels and disciplines and serving as a member of the school's literacy learning team.

It means serving as a technology applications and information literacy leader who works with students at point of instructional need and collaborates in resource planning across the school. Moreover, it means providing professional development to others while consistently continuing to learn oneself. And, finally, it means developing a collection based on student interest and the curriculum and creating programming that draws others into the library media center.

But few administrative preparation programs actually educate future campus leaders and decision makers about library-related "best practice" (MacNeil and Wilson). Consequently, countless library media specialists in elementary and secondary schools spend time "covering classes" during teacher conference periods or faculty absences; trapped in a fixed library schedule or rotation, forced to teach skills out of context and disconnected from the classroom curriculum; managing electronic reading incentive programs; distributing and inventorying textbooks; and supervising a program with no paraprofessional to assist with facilitation. Because the administrative team is instrumental in shaping the roles, responsibilities, and tasks of their campus personnel, they must be more aware of the *appropriate work* of the library media specialist.

That is where this text comes in. This guide is a balance of best practice philosophy and successful application. The intent of this book is not to cover the waterfront of literature on library media programs, nor is it to comprehensively explore all the professional work related to the principalship. Rather, the goal is a balance of both, providing principals with enough substantive information to help them be effective practitioners who understand the impact a well-rounded library media program can have on the learning lives of students and teachers alike. While the primary audience for this book is practicing campus principals and assistant principals, PK–12, it goes without saying that library media specialists at these levels will also have a great deal of interest in this text. A secondary group of interested readers may include those in educational leadership preparation programs at universities and in alternative certification centers, professors planning curriculum for principal preservice programs, curriculum directors and other district-level administrators, and students and faculty in schools of library and information science.

This book provides school leaders with a working knowledge of how to appropriately support the program so that library professionals and their classroom counterparts can practice their expertise, creating a synergistic effectiveness that far exceeds the capabilities of any one person, department, or program. To aid principals, assistant principals, and other school and district leaders in focusing on specific areas of interest and need, this revised edition contains an administrator's self assessment (see Appendix A) for use with each chapter. This tool can be used as a pre- or post-assessment instrument and can help to guide the reader to specific areas of the text or to more in-depth information on particular topics.

About Language and Levels of Practice

In this volume there is no differentiation between secondary and elementary school practices except where there is an obvious or marked difference that will then be noted in the text. Best practice philosophies and concepts can, in general, be implemented and practiced across all schooling levels. Having worked as educators in elementary, middle, and high schools in diverse communities, we believe that this is the most appropriate way to approach the work and to present it here.

The terms *librarian* and *library media specialist*, and *library* and *library media center*, are intended to mean the same thing. And, although the title of *principal* is generally used in reference to the lead administrator on the campus, much of what is presented here is also applicable to assistant, associate, or vice principals. Sometimes the term *campus administrator* is used when the topic or concept is appropriate for anyone who assumes a formal school-level leadership role. In reference to gender-specific language, he and she and him and her are used interchangeably throughout the text.

What Is Included

Each portion of the text is designed to address a critical component of library media services. Every chapter focuses on different aspects of administrator and librarian work and begins with a set of guiding questions an administrator might ask about the themes in that section. Examples and anecdotes of best practice application and collaboration are included throughout to elaborate and illustrate points. After each chapter overview, a list of suggested action steps is offered in order to help principals and other campus leaders get started with developing a quality library media program. Finally, a comprehensive list of additional resources is provided at the close of every chapter to help extend learning to other sources and texts.

Chapter 1 outlines the book's overarching philosophy rooted in instructional leadership, research, and best practice. This chapter focuses on the instructional role of the principal and how that role relates to library media services. Additionally, there is information about a body of research indicating that library media programs affect student performance on a variety of standardized and other learning measures. Also included is a section describing the alignment of information and communications technology skills (ICT skills) with the articulated and taught curriculum. Moreover, to assist school leaders in better understanding the critical aspects of sound library media practice, the most up-to-date national and state standards are also featured.

Chapter 2 presents effective practice in library media centers, beginning with national and state information and communications technology standards for learners. It focuses on the standards recently published by the American Association of School Librarians (AASL). The importance of collaboration between the library media specialist and teachers is followed by the steps to effective collaboration and obstacles that may impede the process. Several instructional scenarios show how teachers and library media specialists work together to deliver quality instruction that integrates ICT skills, along with new technology tools, with content area curriculum. Offered, too, are strategies the library media specialist may use in promoting reading, writing, and visual literacy across the school and curriculum. Next are issues of copyright and plagiarism, highlighting the librarian's probable role.

Chapter 3 targets the varied roles and responsibilities assumed by the library media specialist to ensure that the library media center is integral to the instructional mission of the school. It focuses on the professional roles of the library media specialist—instructional partner, information specialist, literacy programmer, collection developer, and program administrator. Readers will find new sections on the responsibilities of the information specialist, information on developing a culturally responsive collection, and the appropriate uses of reading strategies such as text leveling. This chapter also includes the responsibilities of campus leaders and library media specialists when dealing with challenged books or materials.

Chapter 4 offers guidance for administrators in facilitating tasks specifically related to library media services. These include items such as recruiting and hiring library media center professional and paraprofessional staff, planning for and managing funds related to the librarian and the library media program, building a campus schedule for effective library media use and practice, appropriately allocating learning space, and advocating for strong programs in and outside the school. This chapter concludes with a useful chart outlining administrative actions and decisions that either enable or inhibit library media program practices.

Chapter 5 explains the dual role of the library media specialist as designer and leader of professional development sessions for others and as a professional committed to career-long learning. This section also addresses the characteristics of effective professional development and action research and the role campus administrators play in shaping, supporting, and sustaining adult learning goals and activities. New in this chapter is a process for facilitating two-way communication between the administrative team and the library media specialist. For those schools wishing to assess their library media program, this revised section adds information on conducting a library self study, including companion documents. To assist the library media specialist in improving her practice, a developmental cycle is also included. The GEAR (Gather information, Establish goals, Apply strategies, and Reflect) method can refocus professional practice, help to hone related skills, increase the overall effectiveness of the library media program, and positively affect student performance. The appendixes contain a set of planning guide sheets specific to topics and themes introduced in each chapter. For ease of use, this edition is accompanied by a compact disc (CD), allowing readers and users to conveniently print selected charts, figures, planning or guide sheets, and forms in 8½" × 11" format.

Works Cited

MacNeil, Angus J., and Patricia Potter Wilson. "Preparing Principals for the Leadership Role in Library Media Centers." *Applied Educational Research Journal* 12.2 (2000): 21–27.

CHAPTER 1

Instructional Leadership, Research, and Standards for Library Media Programs

 GUIDING QUESTIONS

What is instructional leadership?

How do instructional leaders support the library media program?

Can the library media program and the library media specialist affect student performance?

What are the national guidelines and state standards for library media programs that help shape best practice?

Introduction

It was the middle of a hot June day, yet learners filled the school library. A middle school principal, the lone administrator in the room, participated in a two-day training seminar alongside the enthusiastic group of teachers and library media specialists from across the district. Participants eagerly learned about a new approach for teaching information literacy.

On the second afternoon of training, a team of elementary teachers and their library media specialist asked a question of the instructor. They wanted advice on how to convince their principal to allow the use of this information search process in their classrooms and library media center during the coming school year. Because their administrator did not have first-hand knowledge about the importance of using such a process and had never been trained in library media center best practice, they feared he would not support the use of such strategies or methods. As the middle school principal listened to the group's comments, she realized just what a significant task it is to hold the title *instructional leader.* How can a principal assist faculty without similar knowledge and training, she thought. Struck by the irony that principals can (and do) impede professional growth and student achievement by discouraging the use of practices unfamiliar to them, she became even more committed to her own career-long learning. Certainly she needed to know what her staff knew if she had any hope of leading a truly effective school.

Practicing instructional leadership is tough, especially in the current atmosphere of increased student testing and accountability. Yet research suggests that instructional leadership is central to creating and maintaining schools that reach and teach all students effectively. A quality library media program supported by strong leadership can enhance teaching and learning for all students on the campus. This chapter focuses on the instructional role of the principal and how that leadership relates to areas such as library media services. Additionally, there is information about how the library media program impacts student performance and the leading national and state standards that guide outstanding library media practice.

Principals and Assistant Principals as Instructional Leaders

There is little doubt that campus administrators are extremely busy people. From making sure buses run on time to monitoring hundreds of students to communicating with parents to ensuring a safe, productive, and healthy environment, school leaders have a lot on their plates. Managing the school well is essential to the survival of this complex organization.

While much of the professional literature about campus leadership targets managing, organizing, and leading, a critical question remains. What are school leaders managing, organizing, and leading for? Principals and assistant principals face tough decisions about how to spend their time. Just like the principal in the training session mentioned earlier in this chapter, campus leaders have to decide what they are going to value and how they are going to behave as instructional leaders. In such a hectic and demanding atmosphere it is challenging to maintain the primary focus of the school—the focus of teaching and learning.

With the introduction of the Effective Schools Correlates by scholars such as Edmonds and Brookover in the 1970s and the second wave of effective schools research in late 1980s, it became clear that the presence of particular factors profoundly affects the learning success of students, regardless of their life situations or the communities in which they live (Glickman, Gordon, and Ross-Gordon).

These factors include the following:

- A clear, focused mission
- Strong principal leadership
- High expectations for students and staff
- Frequent monitoring of student progress
- A positive learning climate
- Parent and community involvement
- An emphasis on student mastery of basic skills

The phrase *strong instructional leadership by the principal* clearly depicts the role of a principal in pursuit of educational excellence, but achieving this goal takes more than an able principal with solid ideas. It requires, instead, a combination of philosophy, knowledge, and action. Practicing instructional leadership means being knowledgeable about and supportive of instructionally sound practices. It means being armed with enough information to fend off gimmicks, fads, or misguided commercial materials in favor of authentic teaching, learning, and assessment. It means empowering others to lead alongside them as part of the educational team. It also means organizing the school so that all faculty, staff, and students can do their best work. Effective instructional leadership is particularly crucial considering the influence of educational accountability systems that require extensive student testing. Such systems can significantly narrow the curriculum and redirect valuable teaching time toward test preparation.

Consider, for instance, the critical area of literacy, the gatekeeper to all other arenas of learning. The principal who is an instructional leader can be a powerful influence in shaping effective literacy learning. In *A Blueprint for Literacy Leadership*, the Children's Literacy Initiative outlined nine areas of content knowledge of principals in fostering literacy on their campuses. These areas are:

- School culture: Principals need to understand the significance of entrenched philosophical and instructional habits that constitute a culture in a school and his or her own power to change that culture.

- Craft leaders: Principals need to know the thinkers and practitioners in the field of literacy instruction who provide fresh ideas and useful models.

- Children's literature: In order to create a community of readers, principals must actively read not only professional literature, but also quality children's literature.

- Instructional models: As the primary filter for new programs, principals must be familiar with a wide range of current instructional models.

- Curricula: The challenge for the principal is to know his or her district's mandated curriculum and make sure teachers are able to deliver it.

- Options for organizing time and space: As the key decision-maker for the use of time and space, principals must be aware of how the use of time and space affects instruction.

- Assessment/content standards: Principals need to know how best to use assessment data that is based on relevant content standards with teachers, school communities, and parents.

- Special interventions: Principals need to take a close look at how support is delivered to struggling students and how this support is organized.

- Knowledge and research: Principals need to know where to find models, data, and organizations that do useful research and that can serve as allies to answer questions of what works and why.

Principals and assistant principals who model successful instructional leadership, therefore, constantly learn about best practices by reading professional books and articles and from a variety of other sources, such as Web sites or online journals. Likewise, they engage in effective supervision activities by visiting instructional settings often and providing substantive feedback for teachers and other professional staff based on the goals and needs of the individual. They attend professional development sessions and participate alongside teachers and staff. And they share instructional leadership activities and duties with others including assistant, associate, and vice principals, team leaders, department heads, and other recognized campus leaders.

Translated into terms of the library media specialist and the library media program, principals and assistant principals who successfully model instructional leadership:

- Constantly learn about best instructional practices in information literacy and the information search process by reading professional books and articles or from a variety of other sources, such as Web sites or online journals. (See "Additional Resources" at the end of this chapter for useful links.)

- Practice effective supervision activities by visiting the library media center and observing the library media specialist, providing substantive feedback based on his or her goals and needs.

- Participate in professional development sessions conducted by the library media specialist, host or attend onsite training by outside experts in this field, and occasionally attend a regional, state, or national conference with the librarian.

- Encourage teachers and the library media specialist to collaborate on integrated instruction, providing time and resources for joint planning and teaching activities.

- Educate others about the importance of the library media center in the learning life of the school and share instructional leadership activities and duties with the entire administrative team including assistant, associate, and vice principals, team leaders, department heads, and other recognized campus leaders, such as the library media specialist.

True instructional leaders strive to understand appropriate indicators of practice not only for classroom teachers but also for other campus professionals such as the librarian, school nurse, counselor, or school psychologist. Understanding the work of these professionals expands the capacity of service on the campus and allows individuals to work more effectively in their trained fields of expertise.

The Library Media Specialist, the Library Media Center, and Student Performance

Educational leaders also need to know how state and local curriculum standards and requirements link to and integrate technology and information literacy skills. As teachers strive to improve student performance on these and other indicators, there is increasing empirical evidence that students in schools with strong library programs perform better. In the article, "Boosting Test Scores," media specialist and department chair Deb Kachel states, "It takes a partnership of administrators, librarians, teachers, parents, and community to build a library program that will make a difference with kids. In this case, it can also help improve reading test scores" (Valenza 6).

Beginning in the early 1990s, an emerging body of research conducted in 19 states and one Canadian province indicated the significance of library media programs to student learning.

> Resource-rich libraries and credentialed school librarians play key roles in promoting both information literacy and reading for information and inspiration. When staffed by qualified professionals trained to collaborate with teachers...school libraries become sophisticated 21st-century learning environments that offer equal opportunities for achievement to all students, regardless of the socio-economic or education levels of the community. (*School Libraries Work!* 1)

In 1993 the Colorado State Library released outcomes of a study called *The Impact of School Library Media Centers on Academic Achievement*. This first Colorado study provided evidence that quality school libraries lead to increased student performance regardless of demographic or economic makeup of the school community. Based on the original findings, a follow-up study was initiated. Lance, Rodney, and Hamilton-Pennell's *How School Librarians Help Kids Achieve Standards* replicated the first inquiry while adding several new perspectives.

In addition to confirming and updating the findings of the first Colorado study, this project expands the original study's results by measuring the impact on academic achievement of:

- Specific leadership and collaboration activities of library media specialists (LMSs)

- Principal and teacher engagement in LM programs

- Information technology, particularly networked computers offering licensed databases and the Internet/World Wide Web (Lance, Rodney, and Hamilton-Pennell 13)

Results of the second study show that reading scores increase as quality characteristics of the library media program increase. When factors such as *program development* (staffing, spending, print and digital titles per student), *information technology* (databases and access to the free Web), *collaboration* (library media specialists planning, teaching, and professionally learning alongside teachers), and *library media center visitation* (number of individual visits per student) rise, so do student performance indicators. In an indirect effect, leadership actions and activities of the library media specialist—meeting with administrators, serving on committees, and working with staff at campus-wide meetings—enhance the working relationship among the library media specialist, teachers, and their students.

EGS Research and Consulting published in April 2001 the results of a study (based on the earlier Colorado works) titled *Texas School Libraries: Standards, Resources, Services, and Students' Performance.* The study had three primary target areas: library resources, services, and use compared to state standards; the impact of school libraries on students' standardized test performance; and library practices common in high-performing schools. Findings indicated that staffing; size of collection; library technology; and teacher, student, and librarian interaction have a positive association with standardized test performance at all schooling levels. Specifically, results showed that students in schools without librarians performed less well on the reading portion of the standardized state examination than students on campuses with librarians. The study also revealed that in schools where teachers and the librarian plan and teach together, student performance is positively impacted.

In several more contemporary studies these earlier findings are reinforced. Lance, Rodney and Hamilton-Pennell found that Indiana students across all grade levels scored better on state exams in schools where principals valued collaborative work between teachers and librarians, supported flexible access scheduling, met on a regular basis with their librarian, and included the library media specialist on important school-level committees. Klinger (2006) discovered that students in schools in Ontario, Canada "with professionally trained school library staff could be expected to have reading achievement scores that were approximately 5.5 percentage points higher than average in grade 6 EQAO [Education Quality and Accountability Office assessment] results" (quoted in *School Libraries Work!* 16).

Supporting the Taught and Tested Curriculum

Using the talents of the library media specialist to integrate information and communications technology skills (ICT skills) within subject-area content also supports and satisfies multiple state-mandated curriculum standards, including those tested on state-level assessments. Consider, for instance, the objectives that are taught when students are writing and using technology within the regular curriculum in English language arts (reading and writing), math, social studies, science, health, languages other than English, or other subject areas. Correlating a research process, including specific ICT skills, and its individual steps with your state's prescribed curriculum standards and skills tested on

INFORMATION AND COMMUNICATIONS TECHNOLOGY SKILLS (RESEARCH PROCESS)	TAKS SOCIAL STUDIES OBJECTIVES FOR GRADE 8
Identify possible sources Choose best sources Locate sources Access information within sources Engage in sources Extract relevant information (summarizing) Organize information from a variety of sources	**The student will use critical-thinking skills to analyze social studies information.** (8.30) **Social studies skills.** The student applies critical-thinking skills to organize and use information acquired from a variety of sources including electronic technology. The student is expected to (A) [differentiate between, locate, and] use primary and secondary sources [such as computer software, databases, media and news services, biographies, interviews, and artifacts] to acquire information about the United States; (B) analyze information by sequencing, categorizing, identifying cause-and-effect relationships, comparing, contrasting, finding the main idea, summarizing, making generalizations [and predictions], and drawing inferences and conclusions; (C) [organize and] interpret information from [outlines, reports, databases, and] visuals including graphs, charts, timelines, and maps; (D) identify points of view from the historical context surrounding an event and the frame of reference which influenced the participants; and (F) identify bias in written, [oral,] and visual material.

Figure 1.1. Correlation between Information Skills and Texas Assessment of Knowledge and Skills (TAKS)

the state's annual performance exam shows that when students engage in a research process they are doing so in a meaningful way. By the very nature of the process, students are interacting with content and skills standards and practicing those tested skills in a meaningful and authentic manner, instead of merely filling out practice worksheets. In Figure 1.1 you will find a correlation of ICT skills and eighth grade tested social studies objectives to use as a model for correlating a research process with your state's academic standards.

National Guidelines and State Standards for Library Media Programs

National guidelines and state standards documents can serve as powerful guides in shaping the work of school library media specialists and in developing and sustaining effective library media programs. *Empowering Learners: Guidelines for School Library Media Programs*, prepared by the American Association of School Librarians (AASL), is an influential source in best library media center practice. Guided by the 2007 *Standards for the 21st-Century Learner* and *Standards for the 21st-Century Learner in Action*, the focus of this text

> has moved from the library as a confined place to one with fluid boundaries that is layered by diverse needs and influenced by an interactive global community. Guiding principles for the school library media program must focus on building a flexible learning environment with the goal of producing successful learners skilled in multiple literacies. (American Association of School Librarians, *Empowering Learners* 5)

See chapter 2 for details about the *Standards for the 21st-Century Learner*.

Empowering Learners can help principals and assistant principals better understand the roles and responsibilities of the library media specialist and the impact the library media center can have school wide. Helpful to the busy school administrator, chapter 1—"Developing Visions for Learning"—discusses the mission of the school library media program, 21st-century skills, the characteristics of the 21st-century learning environment and learner, and summarizes the AASL *Standards for the 21st-Century Leaner*. In this educational paradigm, the library media specialist, once viewed as a staff member who primarily managed resources, should now be considered an active, indispensable member of the instructional team. Included also are the changing roles of the library media specialist. As a leader, teacher, instructional partner, information specialist, and a program administrator, the library media specialist works collaboratively across the campus and the curriculum to help students flourish as learners. (For detailed information about instructional partnerships, see chapter 3 of this text.) "Students must become critical thinkers, enthusiastic readers, skillful researchers, and ethical users of information" (American Association of School Librarians, *Empowering Learners* 18).

Chapter 3 of *Empowering Learners*—"Building the Learning Environment"—is organized around eight guidelines associated with program administration, most needing support of the school's and district's leadership team. This section of the text outlines, in specific terms, the leadership role the library media specialist should assume in building the program and securing administrative (principal) support. These guidelines include:

- Developing a long-term strategic plan reflecting the school's purposes

- Hiring sufficient professional and qualified staff to support the school's instructional programs

- Providing flexible and equitable access to the library's space and resources, supporting the school curriculum and needs of all learners

- Sufficiently funding resources and programs to meet the instructional goals of the school

- Creating policies and procedures that support equitable access to ideas and information

- Developing a collection that reflects the diversity of learners and supports the curriculum

- Developing an advocacy plan that decision makers fully support

- Providing professional development for library media specialists and teachers to further their collaborative efforts (AASL, *Empowering Learners* 29)

Standards for the 21st-Century Learner in Action, a companion to AASL's *Standards for the 21st-Century Learner*, "includes indicators, benchmarks, model examples and assessments to support school library media specialists and other educators in teaching the essential learning skills defined in the learning standards. It also presents action examples for putting the standards into practice in elementary, middle, and high school classrooms" (American Association of School Librarians, "AASL's Newest Publication"). Combined with *Empowering Learners*, this book provides a clear path to planning for and achieving a quality school library media program.

Other excellent resources for sound practice are standards and quality indicator documents published by state departments of education, the state library system, or professional library associations. These publications, generally available via the Internet as well as in hard copy, provide clear direction on topics such as staffing, facilities, resource allocation, collection development, roles and responsibilities, access to and uses of technologies, and curricular and instructional methods. Following are several selected examples from the many publications that are currently available.

The Massachusetts School Library Media Association offers a set of rubrics to use for assessing and improving school library media programs. The instrument provides target indicators under the broad themes of teaching and learning, information access and delivery, and program administration. Each indicator has a set of descriptors across a four-point quality scale from *deficient* on the low end to *exemplary* on the high end. Alongside the library media specialist, campus administrators can use this tool to measure current practice, build on recognized strengths, and target areas in need of improvement.

The Texas State Library & Archives Commission adopted updated school library standards and guidelines in March 2004. The resource packet contains six standards of practice with goals, principles, and a descriptive quality continuum for each standard. Outcome measures and evaluation methods for gauging program effectiveness, a comprehensive glossary of terms, and a list of related professional resources are also included. Principals, assistant principals, and library media specialists can use this document to determine whether their patterns of service are *exemplary* or *below standard*. Likewise, this instrument can prove useful in charting a path to improved practice. (See the "Additional Resources" section at the end of this chapter for an information and retrieval address.)

Other states make their standards documents available in downloadable format from the Internet. These resources, like those already mentioned, are excellent sources of information for school leaders who want to more thoroughly grasp the elements of a model library media program. (See the "Additional Resources" section at the end of this chapter.)

The importance of understanding and applying appropriate standards of service cannot be overstated. A 2007 survey conducted by a school library media specialist in Texas showed that spending on library materials varied greatly from campus to campus, with more than 20 schools in this urban district receiving less than three dollars per student annually to be used for the purchase of library materials ("School Librarians" A6). A similar

2003 study revealed half of the library media centers in a school district were inadequately staffed and 11 lacked the appropriate number of books in their collections. A primary cause cited by district administrators pointed directly to campus leaders. "Part of the problem is the result of site-based management, which gives administrators the authority to allocate their schools' budgets. And with the current emphasis on test scores, schools often cut corners on funding for libraries and the fine arts, district officials told the El Paso Times" ("TX School District" 22).

As informed advocates for best practice, campus leaders can help educate others and use their knowledge to positively guide and shape decision making. An elementary principal in a large, diverse urban school district was called to serve on the district-wide budget council—a representative group of teachers, community members, and campus and district leaders selected to hammer out the district's massive budget and make a recommendation to the school board. In a joint effort with the district's library media director, this principal lobbied for and won a line item in the district budget dedicated specifically to school libraries. In an agreement with upper-level administration, this money—more than one million dollars per year for several years—flowed directly from the district office into campus libraries, bypassing site councils and ensuring that there would be dollars available to library media specialists. This fund was a critical resource in assisting many underfunded school libraries in collection development and in purchasing supplies and needed equipment.

Essential Concepts for This Chapter

This chapter highlights key factors related to leadership, learning, and effective schools. First and foremost, school administrators should be leaders for learning on their campuses. Moreover, this leadership role should extend to the library media center, its staff, and programs. When the library media center is well staffed, funded, and supported by an informed instructional leader, student achievement is positively affected. National guidelines and state standards documents provide excellent guidance in developing effective library media programs.

Planning for Action and Getting Started

1. Read *Empowering Learners* and discuss this document with your library media specialist.

2. Find your state library media standards or guidelines. Secure a copy and read and discuss this information with your librarian.

3. Have a substantive discussion with your library media specialist about his roles, responsibilities, and vision for the library media program.

Works Cited

American Association of School Librarians. "AASL's Newest Publication Helps Put Learning Standards into Practice." *News*. 3 Feb. 2009. American Library Association. 16 June 2009 <http://www.ala.org/=ala/=newspresscenter/=news/=pressreleases2009/=february2009/=aasllearningstandards.cfm>.

American Association of School Librarians. "AASL Standards for the 21st-Century Learner." 2007. <http://www.ala.org/ala/mgrps/divs/aasl/guidelinesandstandards/learningstandards/standards.cfm>.

American Association of School Librarians. *Empowering Learners: Guidelines for School Library Media Programs*. Chicago: American Library Association, 2009.

American Association of School Librarians. *Standards for the 21st-Century Learner in Action*. Chicago: American Library Association, 2009.

Children's Literacy Initiative. *A Blueprint for Literacy Leadership*. 7 July 2004. <http://www.cliontheweb.org/principals_blueprint.html>.

Colorado State Library. *The Impact of School Library Media Centers on Academic Achievement* Denver, CO: Colorado State Library, 1993.

EGS Research and Consulting. *Texas School Libraries: Standards, Resources, Services, and Students' Performance*. Austin, TX: EGS Research and Consulting, 2001.

Glickman, Carl D., Stephen P. Gordon, and Jovita Ross-Gordon. *Supervision and Instructional Leadership*. 8th ed. Boston, MA: Allyn and Bacon, 2010.

Lance, Keith Curry, Marcia J. Rodney, and Christine Hamilton-Pennell. *How School Librarians Help Kids Achieve Standards: The Second Colorado Study*. San Jose, CA: Hi Willow Research & Publishing, 2000.

Massachusetts School Library Media Association. *Model School Rubrics*. Bedford, MA: Massachusetts School Library Media Association, 2002.

"School Librarians: Outdated Books Shelve Learning." *Austin American Statesman* 17 Feb. 2008: A6.

School Libraries Work! Research Foundation Paper. Scholastic Library Publishing, 2008. <http://librarypublishing.scholastic.com/content/stores/LibraryStore/pages/images/SLW3_2008.pdf>

Texas State Library and Archives Commission. *School Library Programs: Standards and Guidelines for Texas*. Austin: Texas State Library and Archives Commission, 14 Aug. 2009. <http://www.tsl.state.tx.us/ld/schoollibs/sls/index.html>.

"TX School District Gives Boost to Libraries." *School Library Journal* 49.9 Sep. (2003): 22.

Valenza, Joyce Kasman. "Boosting Test Scores." *SLJ/Learning Quarterly* 49.12 Dec. (2003): 6.

Additional Resources

Principals as Instructional Leaders

Fink, Elaine, and Lauren B. Resnick. "Developing Principals as Instructional Leaders." *Phi Delta Kappan* 82.8 (2001): 598–606.

Gupton, Sandra Lee. *The Instructional Leadership Toolbox: A Handbook for Improving Practice, 2nd edition*. Thousand Oaks, CA: Corwin, 2009.

Hoerr, Thomas "What Is Instructional Leadership?" *Educational Leadership* 65.4
  (Dec 2007–Jan 2008): 84–85.

Research Studies about Library Media Programs and Performance Outcomes

Champlin, Connie, David V. Loertscher, and Nancy A. S. Miller. *Sharing the Evidence: Library Media Center Assessment Tools and Resources.* San Jose, CA: Hi Willow Research & Publishing, 2008.

Church, Audrey P. *Leverage Your Library Program to Raise Test Scores: A Guide for Library Media Specialists, Principals, Teachers, and Parents.* Columbus, OH: Linworth Publishing, 2003.

Lance, Keith Curry, and David V. Loertscher. *Powering Achievement: School Library Media Programs Make a Difference: The Evidence.* 3rd ed. San Jose, CA: Hi Willow Research & Publishing, 2005.

Loertscher, David V. and Douglas Achterman. *Increasing Academic Achievement through the Library Media Center: A Guide for Teachers.* San Jose, CA: Hi Willow Research & Publishing, 2003.

Nichols, Beverly. *Improving Student Achievement: 50 Research-Based Strategies.* Columbus, OH: Linworth Publishing, 2008.

School Libraries Work! Research Foundation Paper. 3rd ed. Scholastic Library Publishing, 2008. <http://librarypublishing.scholastic.com/content/stores/LibraryStore/pages/images/SLW3_2008.pdf>.

School Library Impact Studies. Library Research Service. 14 Aug. 2009. <http://www.lrs.org/impact.php>.
  This site highlights major research studies and findings linking school libraries and student achievement.

Examples of State Library Media Standards

Minnesota Standards for Effective School Library Programs. MEMO. 14 Aug. 2009. <http://www.memoweb.org/htmlfiles/linkseffectiveslmp.html>.

Standards for Missouri Schools Library Media Centers. Missouri Dept. of Elementary and Secondary Education. 14 Aug. 2009. <http://dese.mo.gov/divimprove/lmc/>.

Utah School Library Media Programs Standards. UELMA, ULMS, and USOE. 14 Aug. 2009. <http://www.usoe.k12.ut.us/curr/library/pdf/standards.pdf>.

CHAPTER 2

Effective Practices in Integrating the Library Media Program Across the School and Curriculum

---

ⓘ **GUIDING QUESTIONS**

What is an information search process and why is this important to principals?

What is collaboration and why should teachers and library media specialists work together?

What is effective curriculum integration?

How can the library media program promote and support literacy?

What are ethical issues involving the library media program?

Introduction

In its ability to span the curriculum, the library media program is a pervasive entity for the mastery of goals and standards, including the promotion of life-long learning and a love of reading. An effective library media program—one that integrates closely with the classroom course of study—will build a community of "critical thinkers, enthusiastic readers, skillful researchers, and ethical users of information" (American Association of School Librarians, *Empowering Learners* 8). Students can meaningfully practice and master almost all state, district, and school curriculum standards through the integration of information and communications technology skills, especially when teachers and library media specialists work together to plan and teach these skills within the context of the subject-area curriculum. State curriculum standards in English language arts and in social studies, and often in other subjects, include information and communications technology skills and may even require that students use an information search process to acquire and use information. Students should easily transfer 21st-century skills—in other words, what library media specialists and teachers have traditionally called research—to all information needs, both academic and personal. "Student research is no longer merely an enrichment activity, but is an important way to learn in preparation for living and working in an information-rich environment" (Kuhlthau 99).

For children to become productive, life-long learners, they should know how to identify when they need information, then successfully use a process through which they figure out their task, acquire and use information efficiently, and effectively show their results, evaluating their efforts at each step of the way. Hopefully, along the way, they are adding value to that knowledge as they process it for meaning. It is in this process and practice that schools turn out information literate citizens. This chapter will show how to integrate the library media program into all areas of the curriculum. Included are national, state, and district learning standards; use of an information search process; collaboration among the library media specialist and teachers; examples of curriculum integration; promotion of reading, writing, and visual literacies; and ethical issues.

Learning Standards

Standardizing the learning of information and technology communications skills ensures that all students, when they leave our high schools, enter higher education or the workforce on the same playing field. Two sets of newly published national standards address not only skills but also the knowledge and attitudes a 21st-century learner must possess to succeed in an increasingly diverse society and global marketplace.

The American Association of School Librarians (AASL) 2007 "Standards for the 21st Century Learner" consists four broad standards:

1. Inquire, think, critically, and gain knowledge
2. Draw conclusions, make informed decisions, apply knowledge to new situations, and create new knowledge
3. Share knowledge and participate ethically and productively as members of our democratic society
4. Pursue personal and aesthetic growth

Included with each standard are four strands of learning: skills, disposition in action, responsibilities, and self-assessment strategies that provide a broad approach to learning the standards. Each strand contains from five to ten observable behaviors, attitudes, and habits. AASL published *Standards for 21st-Century Learner in Action,* a guide to help library media specialists implement the new standards in the school's learning program.

Also in 2007, the International Society for Technology In Education (ISTE) published the *National Educational Technology Standards.* Each of six broad strands in the following list includes four observable behaviors, attitudes, and habits.

1. Creativity and innovation: Students demonstrate creative thinking, construct knowledge, and develop innovative products and processes using technology.
2. Communication and collaboration: Students use digital media and environments to communicate and work collaboratively, including at a distance, to support individual learning and contribute to the learning of others.
3. Research and information fluency: Students apply digital tools to gather, evaluate, and use information.
4. Critical thinking, Problem solving, and decision making: Students use critical-thinking skills to plan and conduct research, manage projects, solve problems, and make informed decisions using appropriate digital tools and resources.
5. Digital citizenship: Students understand human, cultural, and societal issues related to technology and practice legal and ethical behavior.
6. Technology operations and concepts: Students demonstrate a sound understanding of technology concepts, systems, and operations.

In their prescribed student learning standards, state departments of education include a set of information and technology communications skills, usually embedded in the English language arts as research skills. Other subject areas, such as social studies, may also include research skills. Some states have library and information curriculum included as its own subject area in the standards.

Information Search Process

If someone has a problem to solve or a task to accomplish that requires finding and using information, he can, and probably should, use an information search process for this purpose. An information search process is a series of defined steps that provide a systematic method for one to determine the information needed, identify and locate information sources, use those sources, communicate results, and evaluate one's success. When teachers and librarians use an information search process to teach subject area content as well as information and communications technology and other 21st-century skills, students not only engage in the content and skills, they also learn a process that will allow them to transfer school learning to authentic situations.

Many states and individual school districts create their own models for the information search process, or they use or modify one of the popular published models, such as the Big6 Approach to Information and Communications Technology Skills (see "Additional Resources" in this chapter). A school or district may wish to choose one model to implement across grades so that students do not have to learn a new process for each subject or grade. This creates an efficient learning environment for students and saves teachers time because they do not have to teach a new process each year.

Collaboration

Collaboration can be defined as teachers and library media specialists working together to plan, teach, and assess curriculum standards. In their 2002 book, *Increasing Academic Achievement Through the Library Media Center: A Guide for Teachers,* Loertscher and Achterman encourage teachers to use the resources that the library media specialist and the media center have to offer and provide strategies for successful collaboration. Efforts can include planning for reading, writing, and literature appreciation, as well as social studies, science, health, math, other languages, or any subject-area content. Instruction is usually integrated within an information search process framework so that students will learn the information and communications technology skills needed to acquire the content and present their results. Important in the integration of content with process skills is including the component of higher-level thinking and original ideas so that students are required to go beyond the information found in books, Web sites, and other sources. In addition, when students show the results of the information searching, they should gain transferable skills including those of technology, presentation, composition, performance, and production.

Collaborative teams will usually include the library media specialist and one or more classroom teachers in any subject area. Ideally, if the school employs a technology specialist, this teacher will also be included in the team. Additional members may include special education and advanced studies teachers to help plan individualized instruction for students who need an alternative learning experience, bilingual and English as a Second Language teachers, or any combination of teachers. In other words: Who needs to be involved in this planning so that the most effective teaching and learning occurs and every student's needs are best served?

Reasons for Collaboration

Expertise: Bringing the brightest minds together for the sake of teaching and learning makes good sense. Take, for example, a high school coaching staff. Rarely will the school employ only one coach. Typically a school will have a head coach, defensive and offensive coordinators, and a coach of special teams, at the least, and often several more specialists. Knowledgeable and experienced in their fields, the coaches make a team of experts to guide young players in the variety of strategies and skills needed to compete on the field. Let's bring this common practice to the classroom—teachers should not be required to be the sole source of all the information a student needs in a 10-month period. That is a huge responsibility and one that is impossible for any one educator to fulfill, which inadvertently leaves gaps in students' learning. Teaming the library media specialist with the classroom teacher puts the person who is the most knowledgeable about resources and information skills with the person who is the subject-area expert. If the school employs a technology specialist, this teacher brings a rich knowledge of software and Internet applications to assist students in an assortment of end results and products. Since many schools do not employ a technologist, the library media specialist and the teacher will teach the technology skills needed to address the topic. Special education teachers can help to differentiate instruction for all students, especially those with Individual Evaluation Profiles. There are limitless configurations for expert help. Collaboration brings the expertise of individual professionals together for the benefit of the student. These individuals make up the instructional team for a particular curricular unit or set of standards.

Curriculum: Traditionally, many library media specialists taught library skills out of context of the classroom course of study. Teachers brought their classes into the library for instruction on the library's card or on-line catalog or how to use the *Reader's Guide* or encyclopedia indices.

The library media specialist would then have to reteach the skills when students actually needed them for class assignments later in the year.

By planning collaboratively, instruction is a more efficient and effective practice. By using an information search process as the framework for the planning and teaching, many objectives are combined, condensing the amount of time students will spend on each and allowing more time for finding meaning in the content. When skills are taught at the time of need, students make connections between the content area objectives and the information search process, which facilitates the transfer of the information search process to other subjects.

Benefits to Students: One can think about collaboration from the student's point of view. The student sees professionals working together and combining their expertise for his benefit. He sees a synergistic relationship that creates something much greater than any one of the individuals could accomplish alone. When the student has a problem or is stuck wondering which direction to take, he sees more than one professional who is able to help. His needs are met more efficiently, and he is not left to waste time or get lost among the library stacks, so to speak. By interacting with the content through a research process, the student acquires skills to function competently in an information-rich society.

Levels of Collaboration

All teachers and library media specialists experience each level of collaboration as they work with classes throughout a school year (see Figure 2.1 Levels of Collaboration). While full collaboration is desirable when a library media specialist works with a teacher and her class, for a variety of reasons it seems unreasonable to think that it should happen every time. Sometimes, simply aiding a class in checking out books or talking with the class about new or appropriate resources fills the need for the class's visit. English teachers may wish to grade their students' notes and bibliographies, making partial collaboration the perfect fit for that assignment. However, if the library media program has limited or no interaction with students and teachers for a majority of the day, week, month, or year, then the library media specialist and principal will want to conduct action research to find out what it will take to move it forward to more collaborative interactions so that teaching and learning are positively affected (see the GEAR method in chapter 5).

Steps to Effective Collaboration

Planning: Allocating time for planning may be the most important factor for teachers and library media specialists successfully working

No interaction between the library media specialist and teacher. Students come into the library media center to check out books. Library media specialist may help students choose books.

Limited interaction, but no collaboration. Teacher brings class into the library media center to research a topic. No planning occurs between teacher and library media specialist; she helps students on an as-needed or indirect basis.

Beginning collaboration between library media specialist and classroom teacher. Teacher asks library media specialist to talk to students about resources when they come in for research.

Partial collaboration. Teacher and library media specialist plan together. The library media specialist teaches the skills the students need for acquiring information for a curricular unit. Library media specialist not involved in student assessment.

Full collaboration. Teachers and library media specialist plan and teach together. They share teaching of all steps of the information search process, with each presenting to the class her area of expertise. Teachers and library media specialist assist students throughout the duration of the project. The library media specialist is involved in assessment of student process and performance.

Figure 2.1. Levels of Collaboration

together. Using an information problem-solving model such as the ones described previously in this chapter makes the planning fairly straight-forward. Once the content objectives are chosen, the planning team will go through the process step by step, deciding on content and strategies for each step. Using wiki technology or Google Docs, available for free on the Internet, will aide in the planning process, as such tools allow for online collaboration and can result in a one-stop assignment page for students. Teachers and library media specialists can skip the face-to-face planning time and plan as each finds time in her schedule. (See Appendix B for a guide to evaluating a collaborative unit for the library media specialist and teachers to use during collaboration.)

Direct Instruction: During the planning sessions, the team decides which member will assume responsibility for the direct instruction, if needed, during each step of the process. If the library media specialist has a flexible schedule, she is available for teaching information and communications technology skills when students need to know them during the project. Several factors will be considered such as who will teach what, the responsibilities of each while the other is teaching, and how they will work with small groups during instruction. The library media specialist may not always work with the class during each step of the process, but by her involvement in the planning, she knows what has transpired when she interacts with the class.

Assessment of Student Process and Results: Creating a rubric, checklist, or scoring guide together will help the library media specialist and teachers account for students' practice and mastery of curriculum objectives or standards. The assessment instrument is usually given to students as the task is presented during the instructional sequence. By demystifying expectations, students can rise to the standards as they work through the information search process. As often as possible, the library media specialist should assess student results, typically those parts of the instruction she delivered to students including sources used, note taking, Web site evaluation, citing sources, and bibliography construction. The library media specialist's assessment will:

- Emphasize to students that she is a legitimate teaching partner and someone they can rely on for future assistance

- Aide busy teachers in grading, as they will grade the content, leaving the grading of notes, bibliography, and other information skills to the librarian

- Encourage social studies, math, science, industrial arts, second language, and other teachers to add a research component to their curriculum, as they do not have to be knowledgeable in assessing (or teaching) the research skills

- Help her keep track of students' progress in learning information and communications technology skills as defined by the school or district scope and sequence

- Show her which skills she should review to groups or individuals

- Allow her to assess the effectiveness of her instruction

Evaluation: In order to determine the effectiveness of the collaborative process, the team will focus on student performance. This includes information and communications technology skills, as well as learning subject area content. The team may wish to evaluate all steps of the information search process after teaching and assessing the unit of instruction. See Appendix B for an example of an evaluation guide.

Obstacles to Collaboration

Emphasis on Testing: State and national accountability systems and mandated high stakes testing have created a number of unfortunate practices in today's schools. On some campuses, test preparation classes have replaced elective choices for selected groups of students.

In a number of schools, subject areas have completely disappeared because they are not tested curriculum areas. Field-based learning experiences and project-oriented units of study have taken a back seat as instructional time has been redirected to focus on test taking strategies and benchmark assessments. In one district, because the library program was not reflected on the district's educational planning documents, teachers were reluctant to use their instructional time to engage with the librarian media specialist.

Scheduling: A *fixed library schedule,* more common in elementary than in secondary schools, limits or renders impossible the amount of time the library media specialist has to plan and teach a unit with the classroom teacher. A *flexible schedule* allows the teaching to occur at point of need in the grade level's course of study and is critical for this process to have maximum effect on student achievement. See chapter 4 for more information on scheduling options.

Time: The planning process may require one or more sessions, as will the actual teaching of the unit. Members of the instructional team should consider the time they save by combining curriculum objectives (content, technology, and information skills). As students have several opportunities to engage the information search process, their efficiency increases, reducing the amount of time needed to teach those skills students use repeatedly.

Perceptions: Too often, teaching occurs in isolation. Teachers may not be used to another partner in the course of planning and teaching and may be reluctant to share the time they spend with their students. Teachers may view the information search process as an add-on to their curriculum and not see it as an efficient way to have students gain information for that subject. They may feel that they have to "throw the baby out with the bath" by replacing their tried-and-true strategies with new ones. Teachers and library media specialists may be reluctant to work together, with either party concerned that their ideas may be rejected or ridiculed by the other.

Outdated Practices: Traditionally, school libraries served as warehouses for books and teaching materials. The school librarian made these resources available to teachers and students, and promoted literature to all students by reading aloud to classes and offering a variety of programs to encourage students to read. The library program functioned in isolation of the learning that happened in classrooms. While access to books and reading programs remains a top priority of the library media program, it is one of many roles the program should play in teaching and learning. Many school libraries continue to exist outside of, instead of integral to, the instructional mission of the school.

Selected Examples of Full Integration across the Curriculum

The following scenarios illustrate how teachers and the library media specialist collaborated to bring meaningful, developmentally appropriate instruction to students in various grade levels.

Primary Grade Science and Social Studies

A primary grade teacher brings his class into the library to study farm animals. The library media specialist greets them with Maybelle the cow puppet. Maybelle is complaining because she does not understand why she has to go live on a farm when there is delicious grass to eat outside the library and good books to read inside. The librarian assures her that she may still visit the library but that the farm is the best place for cows because the farmer knows how to care for his animals. She tells Maybelle that the children are there to help her learn about living on the farm and about the other animals that will be her friends. The library media specialist and the teacher take turns talking about what the children will do.

The librarian takes the children through the steps of the information search process using Maybelle to sing and help her explain each step to the class. Each pair of students has one farm animal for which they will find answers to questions concerning what it eats, how it is useful to the farmer, how many young it has in a litter, and the proper names for the male, female, and young. Parent helpers (or fifth grade students) work with the students to help them find library books and encyclopedias and use the library's computers with bookmarked or linked Web sites. The children listen and look for answers to their questions as their helpers read relevant passages and show them pictures. With help, they record answers and draw pictures. The teacher and library media specialist talk to each pair as they make a sketch showing a scene that includes the food the animal eats, and the male, female, and the appropriate number of young.

In the computer lab, the technologist (or library media specialist or teacher) shows students how to use the drawing tools in Kid Pix (Bröderbund Software) to recreate their sketch. The teacher helps the students use Kid Pix's voice recorder to describe the way in which the animal is useful to the farmer. The technologist puts the students' pictures together into a slide show titled "Mr. Lander's Class Visits the Farm." Each child evaluates the experience by writing the answers to simple questions such as "what did I learn, what did I learn that I can use again, what did I do well, and did I include all of the information I found out about my animal?" The library media specialist assesses how each group used the information located in sources in its slide and recording.

Intermediate Grade Science

Upper elementary students are studying the biomes of the state, specifically the coastal region. The teachers and the library media specialist work together to introduce the unit. Students, in groups of three or four, will pretend to be marine biologists whose job is to create an exhibit housing a specific marine animal for a public aquarium. The exhibit must include a habitat that supports the animal and display materials so that the public can learn about the animal and its importance to the coastal ecosystem. Each group brainstorms information they will need to find out about their animal, writing these in question form, using Inspiration (Inspiration Software Company) on the computers in the lab, classroom, or library media center. The teacher provides a list of questions required by the state's mandated curriculum. Students notice that they already have some of the questions, so the teacher instructs them to add to the bottom of their list any they do not have.

The library media specialist helps the class create a list of sources and teaches or reviews how to locate and use each. The librarian also teaches a note taking strategy so that students do not copy needless information from the print and electronic sources. Students work in groups to find answers to their questions while the library media specialist, the teacher, and the special education teacher monitor and help as needed.

Once groups have most questions answered (they may not find answers to all of their questions), the teacher leads a discussion about how the exhibits will look. Students decide to make stuffed paper animals and use construction paper, clay, and other materials for the habitats. Word processing or illustration software is used to make informational posters about each animal, its habitat, and its importance to the ecosystem. Students use a scoring guide to ensure that they do not leave out any item of importance in content and format. The library media specialist administers a written student self evaluation and assesses each student's notes for brevity. She sees that many students copied needless information from the sources and makes a mental note to reteach the method when she works with this grade level on a social studies unit next month.

Intermediate Social Studies and Language Arts

The library media specialist and teacher discuss each step of the information search process as they introduce sections of a geography and letter-writing unit to the class. Students studying regions of the United States work for the imaginary U.S. Department of Economic Development. The students' charge is to promote a region of the United States to a company or business that may have a use for the region's plentiful natural resources or may be able to help protect threatened species, diminishing resources, or delicate environments. In their promotional material, students will highlight the major cities and other geographical features that can influence where the company may wish to locate and highlight places of interest and area attractions that will appeal to families. The librarian and teacher help the class brainstorm questions that the groups will need to research about each region, then they put the class in groups and assign each a region. The students put the questions into categories. Each group member takes a category for which he is responsible.

The library media specialist assists the class in determining the best resources for answering their questions and reviews with them how to locate each resource and access the information within. He shows them how to use the keyword search feature on the online catalog and how to use the various search features for the online Student Resource Center (Gale Group, Cengage Publishing). After a note taking review and a brief lesson on how to easily cite sources, students use the sources to answer their questions. The library media specialist and teacher assist and monitor as needed. When students finish, each group compiles its information.

Figuring out which types of companies would most likely benefit from what the region has to offer either by using its natural resources or protecting them, each student in the group chooses a different company. Students use the writing process to compose a letter to the company's CEO providing details about the region and why that corporation may want to locate there. The library media specialist shows the class how to create promotional materials such as pamphlets and brochures using Microsoft Publisher. These will be included with their letters, which give details about area cities, attractions, education, climate, and other items of interest for families that may move with the company. As they write letters and design brochures, the students compare their work to a rubric to determine the standards required for optimum results. Once the project is finished, the librarian has each student fill out a private online self evaluation the library media specialist created using the form feature in Google Docs. The library media specialist assesses the bibliographies and pamphlet design using the information skills section of the rubric.

Middle School Grade Math

For a study of ratios and percents, the math teacher asks the library media specialist to take students through the information search process in order to gather data for analysis and representation with concrete models, fractions, and decimals. They decide that students will work in groups for data gathering and individually for analysis. Students brainstorm surveys that can be conducted around the school, such as students preferring pizza over hamburgers, favorite ice cream flavors, teachers' favorite television shows, or books in the library with the highest number of check outs per year. Some groups use the free survey tool PollDaddy (http://www.polldaddy.com) on laptops they carry around the school. Other groups take surveys by hand and then use spreadsheet tables and charts to analyze the data. The groups compare the analysis and results from each tool and decide which gives the most comprehensive results. Each group then illustrates its results by creating models, fractions, and decimals, then presents its findings to the class by adding its results to a class wiki. Prior to creating their wiki pages, students learned about design principles from the librarian. They evaluate their own efforts by checking their work and writing a summary of the experience to turn in with their spreadsheets. The library media specialist helps the teacher assess students' final wiki pages, looking for evidence of effective design principles.

Middle School Health

In a study of Human Immunodeficiency Virus (HIV) infection and sexually transmitted diseases, the teacher and library media specialist create an activity that has students playing the role of scriptwriter for their favorite television show. Each group of students chooses from a list of sexually transmitted diseases. They write an episode for their favorite network TV program, weaving into the storyline information about the disease, its symptoms, the possible cures or treatments, and the consequences characters experience because of their lifestyle choices. Since this is for network TV, the script has to be appropriate for family viewing. The teacher and library media specialist introduce the unit together, using appropriate terminology for each step of the information search process and answering questions from the excited class. Groups brainstorm information that each will need to find out about its disease. Since the library's collection of health books is somewhat dated, subscription databases and selected free Web sites will be introduced by the library media specialist. She reviews the various search features and the library's printing policy. She also instructs them in Web site evaluation, cautioning students about questionable health sites. She requires that students turn in evaluations for each site that they use that she did not provide. Students understand that they should copy and paste sections from Web sources to a word processor instead of printing entire Web sites.

The teacher instructs the class on efficient note taking and allows them to begin their research. The library media specialist and teacher walk from group to group, helping as needed. When students finish taking notes, the language arts teacher works with them on drafting a script for their episode of the television show. She instructs them in dialogue writing and authentic voice. Students understand that they must choose a favorite show that lends itself to this type of content. Students must add, in a serious manner, the information they've located about their disease. The groups write a final version of the show (of course, it is not exactly the same length as a real episode).

As a conclusion, each group presents a readers' theater. The librarian and teacher film each group, which then edits its own video and uploads it to TeacherTube (http://www.teachertube.com). As the class watches the videos, each student fills in a chart that will compare and contrast each disease. They use the chart to study for a quiz. The library media specialist creates an informal written self evaluation on the experience for individual students to complete and assesses the students' Web evaluations.

High School Social Studies and Language Arts

In studying *Hamlet*, the history teacher explains the importance of understanding the society in which Shakespeare belonged and how it might have influenced his writing. This gives students a deeper background in which to appreciate and comprehend Shakespeare's writing and the time in which the play was performed. Students transport themselves to Elizabethan England in 1600. Each assumes a role from a list given by the teacher, such as 14-year-old male apprentice to the Globe organization, Shakespeare himself, 10-year-old daughter of a tavern keeper next to the Globe, 50-year-old merchant who is a patron of the Globe and of Shakespeare, Sir Walter Raleigh, and others. The student is responsible for writing a journal entry in which he reveals what his character did on that date. Students will refer in some way to the production of the new play, *Hamlet*, and also reflect the daily routine of their lives in England near 1603 and the death of Queen Elizabeth.

The library media specialist shows students the history databases to which the library subscribes, in addition to print resources and sites on the free Web. Journal entries from various historical time periods complete the list of sources. Students learn how to use the school's Web site evaluation guide that requires them to assess each site that they find on their own. The librarian instructs students on how to access and use a note taking organizer she created using Microsoft Word. The students seem enthusiastic to have such an organizer and are especially grateful when she demonstrates NoodleBib, simplifying the tradition-ally tedious job of citing sources. After a short session on plagiarism, students understand the importance of citing sources when they quote, summarize, or paraphrase.

Students research life in Elizabethan England in 1600, taking notes and reading authentic journal entries to understand the proper format. When they finish researching their subjects, they draft their journal entries, revise, and write the final entry, attempting their best cursive script. Some students get creative with the type of paper they use for the journal, trying to simulate parchment. As they write, they use the rubric provided by their teacher to meet his expectations. Students turn in notes, Web site evaluations if needed, and all drafts of their work. The library media specialist assesses their note taking skills and works cited lists, while the history teacher assesses the journal entries.

High School Art History

To demonstrate their mastery of concepts at the end of a unit on 20th-century American art, the art history teacher collaborates with the library media specialist to design an activity that will authentically assess students' knowledge. They develop a unit of instruction that the juniors will enjoy and will work on with enthusiasm.

They set the stage with a scenario about a foundation, endowed by a wealthy American oilman and World War II veteran, that awards a large monetary prize each year to an art museum to expand its collection of 20th-century American art. Each student pretends to be the curator of an art museum who wants to obtain the grant from the Foundation in order to expand its collection. His task is to present a group of six paintings from the 20th century to the Board of Trustees of the Founda-tion to show that, as the museum's curator, he has the ability to collect works that adhere to the mission statement of the Foundation. He must convince the Board that his museum is worthy of the Foundation's grant monies and that his expertise in collecting will fulfill the goals for their Foundation. The curator knows that the award will be made on how closely his museum's collection fits the mission statement of the Foundation. Students understand that the successful entry will have a clear statement of purpose of its collection; it will have a minimum of six works of art from at least three different schools; entrants will identify the painting by title, artist, date, and current location; entrants will explain why the work is in the museum, how it has been influenced by other art, how it influences art, and how it relates to American culture. Students use Web sites provided by the teacher and library media specialist as well as books and subscription databases, such as *Grove Dictionary of Art* (Oxford University Press) from the library's online collection. They will use PowerPoint or Animoto (http://www.animoto.com) to display the art works in a presentation for the Board of Trustees. As they view each other's presentations, class members take notes and hand in a one-page analysis of four presentations in which each student grades the presentations on the evaluation guidelines provided and explains briefly why she has given them the grade. Each student selects a winner of the Foundation's prize and clearly articulates why she chose that entrant.

The library media specialist has a minimal role in actually teaching this activity. After planning with the teacher, she locates appropriate Web resources, subscription databases, and library books. She makes the activity into a Web page for the school's library Web site with active links to Web resources. Students ask for guidance in the use of Web resources and library materials, and she helps as requested. She assesses their bibliographies.

High School Environmental Science and English Composition

In determining whether the imaginary Transcontinental Pipeline Company's proposal is a financial windfall or an environmental disaster, students assume one of three roles: a biologist, an environmental expert, or a spokesman for the pipeline company. The teacher and library media specialist designed the following scenario for the class: A pipeline company is proposing to lay a crude oil pipeline through the western part of the county. Its line will have to go through property behind their school. Save Our Habitat, an environmental group, is opposing the pipeline. Transcontinental Pipeline Company is offering a large financial incentive to the school district for the endorsement of the school board when the project is debated before the city council. The school board has set a hearing so that they can get all the facts before they make a decision on whether or not to include their name on an endorsement of the project when it is debated before the

City Council. They have invited a biologist to testify on environmental issues of the area, a representative from Save Our Habitat, and a spokesperson from the pipeline company.

Students are put in groups of three and assigned a role to assume. Biologists will study the habitat along the proposed line on the property. They need to determine the effects of the line on the habitat and the impact on the flora and fauna, including threatened and endangered species. Environmentalists will make arguments opposing the pipeline because of its negative impact on the habitat and the potential hazard to the community. They will also look at the effects of surface water pollution, ground water pollution, and on the aquifer recharge zone. Pipeline company spokespersons will need to have knowledge of how the pipeline goes in and its benefits to the school, in order to convince the Board that the pipeline will have no adverse effects on the environment or the community. They will have to obtain compliance with the National Pollutant Discharge Elimination System, including the completion of a Storm Water Pollution Prevention Plan.

With their teacher's help, groups brainstorm information they will research for their roles. The library media specialist prepares a list of Web site links and reviews the search features of the science databases to which the library subscribes. He reminds students to cite sources, if needed. Students take field notes and organize them using a word processor. Each group prepares a slide show or video for its presentation to the school board. As each group presents, students takes notes in order to write an editorial for the newspaper giving the paper's opinion on whether or not the school should endorse the project. From the English teacher, students learn how to write an editorial. Using a rubric provided by their teachers and library media specialist, students self evaluate their work before turning it in. The teachers assess for content, and the library media specialist grades the process and bibliography. Each student receives a group grade and an individual grade for the editorial.

Promoting Reading, Writing, and Visual Literacy

The library media specialist promotes reading, writing, and visual literacy through engaging programs and integrated instruction and by developing a collection of print and electronic resources to meet the academic and personal needs of students. Print resources will include award-winning and current literature and an assortment of magazines of interest to students. Electronic resources may include a streaming video service, such as Discovery Streaming, and an assortment of videos or DVDs. The library media specialist previews and purchases subscription databases for teacher and student use. Many state departments of education (or other agencies) provide access to quality subscription databases at reduced or no additional costs to schools.

To promote literacy, librarians bring storytellers and authors to students in all grade levels. They create developmentally appropriate and meaningful writing, viewing, and listening activities for holidays and ethnic celebrations. Primary students may flock to the library media center to see a toad in a terrarium or file through each day checking on the progress of chicken eggs that will hatch, and then borrow fiction and nonfiction books about toads or chickens. Middle school students may sit on the floor of the library listening to a published poet, then return to class and compose their own poetry. Writing a letter to an author, living or deceased, may motivate high school students to read from a variety of literature. Blogs promoting new books, book club selections, and other literature-related news keep students repeatedly visiting their library's Web site for good book suggestions. Student-created podcasts for the library Web site promoting new books or those from a list of censored books for Banned Books Week can motivate even reluctant teens. Librarians market their state library association's annual reading list to their students and help promote their state library's summer reading program. There are countless ways the library media specialist inspires children to practice the skills needed to write, read, and view intelligently.

Ethical Issues and the Library Media Program

Citizens in a democratic society should have the ability to physically and intellectually access ideas and information from a variety of viewpoints. In return, citizens have the responsibility of using the ideas and information ethically and responsibly. The library media program should support those ideals for its students.

Promoting Intellectual Freedom through the Library Media Program

The American Library Association's "Library Bill of Rights," adopted in 1948, provides guiding principles for the services of libraries so that they are "forums for information and ideas." These principles ensure that libraries provide citizens with materials presenting information on all points of view and that support the "interests, information, and enlightenment of all people the community serves." In addition, libraries should challenge censorship and not deny anyone's right to use the materials and space based on "origin, age, background, or views."

How does the *Library Bill of Rights* affect school libraries? "Although the educational level and program of the school necessarily shape the resources and services of a school library media program, the principles of the *Library Bill of Rights* apply equally to all libraries, including school library media programs" (American Association of School Librarians, *Empowering Learners* 53). An effective library media program supports all principles of intellectual freedom.

Equal Access to Ideas and Information

All students have the right to physically and intellectually access ideas and information for personal and academic needs. The library media center should contain high-quality print and online resources, including those that support the language needs of the majority of the community it serves. As school populations become even more diverse, the library collection should reflect this rich diversity. These materials must be physically accessible for all students, and the library media specialist should instruct students so that they have the information and communications technology skills needed to intellectually make meaning from the ideas in the resources.

Physical access constitutes placement of print and online resources so that all students, including those who have disabilities, can obtain needed materials. It also includes teaching students how to physically locate those materials, such as the use of the library's online public access catalog and the arrangement of materials on the shelves. It will also require teaching students how to identify and locate those electronic databases and Web sites that are appropriate for their topics and levels of cognitive development.

Blocking access to Internet tools such as wikis, blogs, and other participatory Web sites stifles creativity, communication, and collaboration among faculty and students. Most of these tools allow students to publish to an authentic audience, as well as share and collaborate ideas and information with their teachers and peers inside and outside the classroom. It extends the confines of the 45-minute class period and encourages *all* students to participate in written discussion. Wikis, blogs, and other appropriate social networking platforms have settings that can be set to restrict outsiders from reading, commenting, or joining. These tools can be customized for safety and privacy for use in the classroom. Administrators whose schools' or districts' information technology staff block access to these tools will want to educate the staff on their fine educational merit and allow access to teachers, and possibly students.

Not all students have online access at home or live close to a public library, so the school administration and library media specialist may consider, if staffing and funding is available, extending the school library's hours of operation to accommodate students before and after school. For those students who do have online availability at home, library media specialists negotiate with publishers to provide remote access to subscription databases and then inform students of those logins and passwords. Librarians may also want to host virtual office hours through instant messaging, e-mail, and other communication tools to assist students during projects on which the library media specialist and teacher have collaborated.

Intellectual access to information requires that students know how to find relevant information within sources, make meaning from it, and incorporate it into their existing body of knowledge. The library media specialist works with students, in the context of their classroom and personal needs, to teach these information skills at a developmentally appropriate level and may do so within the framework of an information search process.

Copyright and Plagiarism

The faculty member with the most knowledge about copyright and plagiarism is usually the library media specialist. He instructs the faculty on copyright issues as they apply to the classroom and the use of instructional materials but does not assume the role of "copyright cop" for the faculty. Enforcement of copyright is the responsibility of the principal. If a faculty member is in violation of copyright, the library media specialist may inform the principal, who should then confront the teacher. School administrators must be aware of copyright and Fair Use Guidelines as they apply to education and model those practices in their use of materials with faculty. Carol Simpson's *Copyright for Administrators* (Linworth Books) will provide busy principals with the basics of copyright.

Plagiarizing and cheating seem to be pervasive throughout schools in the nation, with the practice increasing as students progress through the grades. No school is immune to violations. Students must understand that with the right to have access to information comes the responsibility of using it ethically. One of the most effective ways of teaching about copyright and plagiarism and setting expectations for students is through its integration into the content area curriculum, where students will have a need for learning about these two concepts. The library media specialist may want to develop a presentation for classes and offer to present a lesson on the concepts before a class works on an assignment that may lend itself to a violation of copyright or may be easily plagiarized. She can also work with teachers on implementing effective strategies to try to eliminate plagiarism in their classes.

Essential Concepts for This Chapter

By working together to integrate content with information and communications technology skills, library media specialists and teachers have enormous potential to ensure student success. By using an information search process as a framework for teaching and learning, outcomes for students are powerful. Students gain an increasing awareness of how to work cooperatively, the ability to spend more time finding meaning instead of skimming the surface of individual content area objectives, and acquire a set of skills to function successfully in a society overwhelmed with information. The librarian promotes reading, writing, and visual literacy in a variety of ways. The library media specialist also develops programs and strategies for the campus that include access to a wide range of information and teach ethical behavior in using that information.

Planning for Action and Getting Started

1. Work with the library media specialist and a team of teachers to select an information search process to implement across the grade levels at your school. Provide training to faculty if needed.

2. Study the state and district standards for information and communications technology skills.

3. For the benefit of students, encourage teachers and the library media specialist to collaborate as often as possible.

4. Ask your library media specialist if a range of viewpoints (as appropriate) is represented in print and online.

5. Work with the library media specialist to determine if all students have physical and intellectual access to information.

6. Meet with district- or building-level technology personnel to ensure that access is provided to Web tools that promote teaching and learning, such as wikis and blogs.

7. Have a focused conversation with your library media specialist about ways he is promoting reading, writing, and visual literacy across the grades.

8. Ask your library media specialist to present copyright laws and Fair Use Guidelines at a faculty meeting and stress that teachers are required to adhere to them. Talk to the faculty about combating issues of student plagiarism, as appropriate for each grade level.

Works Cited

American Association of School Librarians. *Empowering Learners: Guidelines for School Library Media Programs.* Chicago: American Library Association, 2009.

American Association of School Librarians. "AASL Standards for the 21st-Century Learner." 2007. <http://www.ala.org/ala/mgrps/divs/aasl/guidelinesand standards/learningstandards/standards.cfm>.

American Association of School Librarians. *Standards for the 21st-Century Learner in Action.* Chicago: American Library Association, 2009.

American Library Association. "Library Bill of Rights." *Issues and Advocacy.* American Library Association, 24 Jan. 1996. 6 Feb 2009. <http://www.ala.org/ala/ issuesadvocacy/intfreedom/librarybill/index.cfm>.

International Society for Technology in Education. "NETS for Students 2007." *National Educational Technology Standards.* International Society for Technology in Education, 2007. 3 Feb. 2009. <http://www.iste.org/Content/ NavigationMenu/NETS/ForStudents/2007/Standards/NETS_for_ Students_2007.htm>.

Kuhlthau, Carol Collier. "The Process of Learning from Information." *The Virtual School Library.* Ed. Carol Collier Kuhlthau. Englewood, CO: Libraries Unlimited, 1996. 95–104.

Loertscher, David V., and Douglas Achterman. *Increasing Academic Achievement through the Library Media Center: A Guide for Teachers.* San Jose, CA: Hi Willow Research & Publishing, 2002.

Simpson, Carol. *Copyright for Administrators.* Columbus, OH: Linworth Publishing, 2008.

Additional Resources

Information Search Process and Information Literacy

American Association of School Librarians. "AASL Standards for the 21st-Century Learner." 2007. <http://ala.org/ala/mgrps/divs/aaslproftools/learningstandards/ AASL_LearningStandards.pdf>.

American Association of School Librarians."Learning4Life: A National Plan for Implementation of *Standards for the 21st Century Learner* and *Empowering Learners: Guidelines for School Library Media Programs.*" 2009. <http:// www.ala.org/aasl/learning4life>.

Callison, Daniel, and Leslie Preddy. *The Blue Book on Information Age Inquiry, Instruction and Literacy.* Westport, CT: Libraries Unlimited, 2006.

Eisenberg, Michael B., Carrie A. Lowe, and Kathleen L. Spitzer. *Information Literacy: Essential Skills for the Information Age.* Englewood, CO: Libraries Unlimited, 2004.

Eisenberg, Michael B., and Laura Eisenberg Robinson. *The Super3: Information Skills for Young Learners.* Columbus, OH: Linworth Publishing, 2007.

Jansen, Barbara A.. *The Big6 Goes Primary!: Teaching Information and Communications Technology Skills in the K-3 Curriculum.* Columbus, OH: Linworth Publishing, 2009.

Jansen, Barbara A. *The Big6 in Middle School: Teaching Information and Communications Technology Skills.* Columbus, OH: Linworth Publishing, 2007. Kuhlthau,

Carol Collier, Leslie K. Maniotes, and Ann K. Caspari. *Guided Inquiry: Learning in the 21st Century*. Westport, CT: Libraries Unlimited, 2007.

Murray, Janet R. *Achieving Educational Standards Using the Big6*. Columbus, OH: Linworth Publishing, 2008.

National Forum on Information Literacy. 09 May 2009. <http://www.infolit.org>.

Needham, Joyce. *Teaching Elementary Information Literacy Skills with the Big6*. Columbus, OH: Linworth Publishing, 2008.

Riedling, Ann Marlow. *An Educator's Guide to Information Literacy: What Every High School Senior Needs to Know*. Westport, CT: Libraries Unlimited, 2007.

Collaboration

Buzzeo, Toni. *Collaborating to Meet Standards: Teacher/Librarian Partnerships for K-6*. 2nd ed. Columbus, OH: Linworth Publishing, 2007.

Buzzeo, Toni. *Collaborating to Meet Standards: Teacher/Librarian Partnerships for K-2*. Columbus, OH: Linworth Publishing, 2007.

Buzzeo, Toni. *Collaborating to Meet Standards: Teacher/Librarian Partnerships for 7–12*. Worthington, OH: Linworth Publishing, 2002.

Buzzeo, Toni. *The Collaboration Handbook*. Columbus, OH: Linworth Publishing, 2008.

Harada, Violet H., Carolyn H. Kirio, and Sandra H. Yamamoto. *Collaborating for Project-Based Learning for Grades 9–12*. Columbus, OH: Linworth Publishing, 2008.

Harada, Violet H., and Joan M. Yoshina. *Inquiry Learning through Librarian-Teacher Partnerships*. Worthington, OH: Linworth Publishing, 2004.

Harker, Christa, and Dorette Putonti. *Library Research with Emergent Readers: Meeting Standards through Collaboration*. Columbus, OH: Linworth Publishing, 2008.

Moreillon, Judi. *Collaborative Strategies for Teaching Reading Comprehension: Maximizing Your Impact*. Chicago: American Library Association, 2007.

Volkman, John D. *Collaborative Library Research Projects: Inquiry That Stimulates the Senses*. Westport, CT: Libraries Unlimited, 2008.

Curriculum Integration

Bishop, Kay. *Connecting Libraries with Classrooms: The Curricular Roles of the Media Specialist*. Worthington, OH: Linworth Publishing, 2003.

Harvey, Carl A. *No School Library Left Behind: Leadership, School Improvement, and the Media Specialist*. Columbus, OH: Linworth Books, 2008.

Loertscher, David V., Carol Koechlin, and Sandi Zwaan. *Beyond Bird Units! Thinking and Understanding in Information-Rich and Technology-Rich Environments*. San Jose, CA: Hi Willow Research and Publishing, 2007.

Miller, Donna. *The Standards-Based Integrated Library: A Collaborative Approach for Aligning the Library Program with the Classroom Curriculum*. 2nd ed. Worthington, OH: Linworth Publishing, 2004.

Stripling, Barbara K., and Sandra Hughes-Hassell, eds. *Curriculum Connections through the Library*. Englewood, CO: Libraries Unlimited, 2003.

Villa, Richard. *A Guide to Co-teaching: Practical Tips for Facilitating Student Learning*. Thousand Oaks, CA: Corwin Press, 2004.

Ethical Issues

Adams, Helen R. *Ensuring Intellectual Freedom and Access to Information in the School Library Media Program*. Westport, CT: Libraries Unlimited, 2008.

American Library Association. "Freedom to Read Statement." 30 June 2004. <http://www.ala.org/ala/aboutala/offices/oif/statementspols/ftrstatement/freedomreadstatement.cfm>.

Crews, Kenneth D. *Copyright Law for Librarians and Educators: Creative Strategies and Practical Solutions*. 2nd ed. Chicago: American Library Association, 2005.

Hoffman, Gretchen McCord. *Copyright in Cyberspace 2: Questions and Answers for Librarians*. New York: Neal-Schuman Publishers, 2005.

Hopkins, Janet. "School Library Accessibility: The Role of Assistive Technology." *Teacher Librarian* Feb. (2004): 15–18.

Johnson, Doug. *Learning Right from Wrong in the Digital Age: An Ethics Guide for Parents, Teachers, Librarians, and Others Who Care About Computer-Using Young People*. Worthington, OH: Linworth Publishing, 2003.

Preer, Jean. *Library Ethics*. Westport, CT: Libraries Unlimited, 2007.

Scales, Pat R. *Protecting Intellectual Freedom in Your School Library*. Chicago: American Library Association, 2009.

Lathrop, Ann, and Kathleen Foss. *Student Cheating and Plagiarism in the Internet Era: A Wake-up Call*. Englewood, CO: Libraries Unlimited, 2000.

Lathrop, Ann, and Kathleen Foss. *Guiding Students from Cheating and Plagiarism to Honesty and Integrity: Strategies for Change*. Westport, CT: Libraries Unlimited, 2005.

Russell, Carrie. *Complete Copyright: An Everyday Guide for Librarians*. Chicago: American Library Association, 2004.

Simpson, Carol, with Christine Weiser, ed. *Copyright for Administrators*. Columbus, OH: Linworth Publishing, 2008.

Simpson, Carol. *Copyright for Schools: A Practical Guide*. 4th ed. Columbus, OH: Linworth Publishing, 2005.

Simpson, Carol. *Ethics in School Librarianship: A Reader*. Worthington, OH: Linworth Publishing, 2003.

Promoting Reading, Writing, and Visual Literacy

Beers, Kylene. *When Kids Can't Read: What Teachers Can Do, a Guide for Teachers 6–12*. Portsmouth, NH: Heinemann, 2003.

Grimes, Sharon. *Reading Is Our Business: How Libraries Can Foster Reading Comprehension*. Chicago: American Library Association, 2006.

Halsall, Jane, and R. William Edminister. *Visual Media for Teens: Creating and Using a Teen-Centered Film Collection*. Westport, CT: Libraries Unlimited, 2009.

Krashen, Stephen D. *The Power of Reading: Insights from the Research*. 2nd ed. Westport, CT: Libraries Unlimited, 2009.

Warlick, David F. *Redefining Literacy 2.0*. 2nd ed. Columbus, OH: Linworth Publishing, 2009.

CHAPTER 3

Understanding the Roles and Responsibilities of the Library Media Specialist

 GUIDING QUESTIONS

What are the most important roles of the library media specialist?
What are additional major responsibilities?
How are these responsibilities fulfilled?
How can a library collection reflect a diverse student population?
When books or instructional materials are challenged, what should the principal do?
How should library media specialists prioritize their time for the learning and achievement of students?

Introduction

In implementing the national guidelines and state standards for a quality library media program, the library media specialist assumes many roles and takes on dozens of responsibilities, ensuring that students and faculty have access to an effective program. Four major professional roles of the library media specialist include: partnering with classroom teachers and others for effective instruction; connecting students and teachers to technologies that support the school's curriculum and connect them to the global learning community; fostering literacy by guiding readers to quality books that serve their interests and needs; and developing a quality collection of physical and online resources. Additional responsibilities that fall under the fifth role, that of program administrator, may include, but are not limited to:

- Evaluating the program against the national and state's standards for school library media programs

- Providing staff development for faculty

- Promoting safe and ethical Internet use

- Analyzing data and reporting statistics

- Serving as a resource to teachers and students by gathering materials and online resources, and in creating online pathfinders of books and digital resources for upcoming assignments and projects

- Preparing and maintaining a budget for capital purchases and operating expenses

- Attending grade level or departmental meetings to communicate the goals of the program and collaborate with teachers

- Providing access to materials

- Instructing students in the arrangement of the library and the use of the online catalog

- Acquiring and managing the library's, and sometimes the school's, technology resources, such as digital video recorders and cameras

- Maintaining the library's virtual presence such as the Web page, blog, or wiki

- Keeping current on emerging technologies

- Orienting students and faculty to library services and facilities

- Developing and maintaining a volunteer program

- Communicating with public libraries that serve the school's attendance area

While not at all comprehensive, these are the library media specialist's main responsibilities. Other important administrative duties consist of, but are not limited to, supervising paraprofessionals and volunteers, short- and long-term goal setting, engaging in public relations activities (see "Advocacy for the Library Media Program" in chapter 4), checking out materials to students and faculty, maintaining the library's physical space, promoting the collection to parents, and conducting a systematic inventory of all library materials and equipment. The library media specialist will also prepare annual reports, coordinate the school's use of regional educational service center instructional materials, order and maintain equipment and supplies (lamps, blank CDs, etc.), train students and faculty in the use of multimedia software and equipment, provide access to publishers' catalogs, acknowledge receipt of gift items, order and provide access to a periodicals collection for students and staff, repair damaged books, and remove old and damaged books and materials. The librarian will most likely participate in professional organizations and various extracurricular activities in the school, as well as read literature in and out of the school library field.

Under the supervision of the library media specialist, a paraprofessional can assume some of the duties described. Of course, not all libraries have a paraprofessional. In such cases, all duties will be assumed by the library media specialist, and hopefully a cadre of parent, student, or community volunteers.

Instructional Partnership

Inherent to an effective library media program is a library media specialist who functions first and foremost as a partner in the planning for and teaching of national, state, and local curriculum standards. These standards, as the building principal knows, are the heart of the instructional program. It is the mastery of these standards by which students are assessed and schools evaluated. While some information and technology skills are not assessed on state standardized tests, it is the mastery of these skills that will make students successful and productive in the workplace. A student who demonstrates proficiency in information and communications technology skills, as well as content objectives, should experience success in many areas of life. Someone who knows how to learn for a lifetime knows how to find out what she does not know. She can recognize a problem, locate the information needed to solve it, and use the information in a creative or critical way. She is curious and excited about the world and initiates her own learning and possesses the 21st-century skills to do this. The library media specialist plays a major role in the creation of an information-literate community by collaborating with teachers to integrate information and technology curriculum standards with those in subject areas.

Empowering Learners, by the American Association of School Librarians, describes this role as:

> The SLMS [school library media specialist] collaborates with classroom teachers to develop assignments that are matched to academic standards and include key critical thinking skills, technology and information literacy skills, and core social skills and cultural competencies. The SLMS guides instructional design by working with the classroom teacher to establish learning objectives and goals, and by implementing assessment strategies before, during, and after assigned units of study. In a 24–7 learning environment, communication with classroom teachers and students now takes place virtually, as well as face-to-face. (American Association of School Librarians 17)

Imperative in the professional development of the principal and the library media specialist and in the effective development of content area curriculum within the framework of the library media program is the reading and implementation of *Empowering Learners: Guidelines for School Library Media Programs*, as mentioned in chapter 1. If the principal encourages teachers to collaborate with the library media specialist to integrate information and communications technology skills in the subject-area curriculum, the school will almost certainly see enormous gains in student achievement. For a detailed account about *Empowering Learners*, see the national guidelines and state standards section in chapter 1. Find information about collaboration and examples of information and communications technology skills integration across the curriculum in chapter 2.

Information Specialist

A library media specialist also serves as the school's Chief Information Officer. Her role as information specialist spans a wide range of resources and systems. She must acquire an extensive knowledge and collection of free and fee-based on-shelf and online resources and help students and teachers identify, access, evaluate, and use them effectively. She keeps current in emerging technologies and in new ways to use common technology tools, and helps teachers identify ways to use them in their content areas and teaches students how the tools can help them effectively communicate the results of information searching. The information specialist helps students and teachers set up a personal Web page such as iGoogle, NetVibes, or Pageflakes that contains a variety of widgets, or applications, that include easy access to e-mail, calendar, to-do list, daily news, current weather conditions, calculator, and a host of other useful tools and data. She shows teachers and administrators how to use an aggregator to collect RSS feeds in one site for those Web pages and blogs they must visit frequently for new and updated information, saving them time and energy. She provides access to and expertise in using participative tools such as blogs, wikis, and social networks that help connect stakeholders to a global learning community, while ensuring that their privacy is protected and that the tools are used in a safe and ethical manner. Promoting ethical use of ideas and information through education about copyright laws, fair use of copyrighted materials, and avoidance of plagiarism by proper attribution, she stays current in laws, guidelines, and strategies to accomplish this important goal. The specialist uses technology tools to extend the library media services and resources beyond the walls and hours of the facility, allowing students to request assistance and access resources at point of need. The information specialist works with administrators and teachers to develop curriculum that effectively integrates information and communications technology skills so that students enter college or the workplace possessing the attitudes and skills of a 21st-century learner.

In the library media program, technology has several roles: (1) to connect students and faculty to ideas and information and to help them use tools to communicate the results of information searching, (2) to connect students and faculty to a global learning community, (3) to automate and extend access to materials, and (4) and to allow the library media specialist to communicate with colleagues, increase productivity, and access professional resources, similar to the way a principal would use technology. Additionally, technology can be made available in the library to students for productivity such as word processing and multimedia development. The library media specialist assumes the responsibility of training faculty and students how to use the library's, and often the school's, available technology for information access and productivity. *Empowering Learners* states that "the SLMS [school library media specialist] introduces and models emerging technologies...He or she is a leader in software and hardware evaluation, establishing the processes for such evaluation to take place" (American Association of School Librarians 17). If the librarian's computer is in her office, it should have the capability to bypass the school's Internet content filter so she can have unrestricted access to ideas and information. At the very least, she should have the authority to unblock Web sites as needed.

Nurturing a good working relationship with the technology support department goes a long way in keeping the library computers and network up-to-date, functional, and available for students and faculty. The library media specialist and the technology staff should work closely together to provide the unrestricted and rapid access to the best resources for the teachers and students.

Automating Access to Materials

Purchasing decisions related to library automation (electronically accessing materials housed in the school library and beyond) falls directly under the library media specialist's domain and is supported by the principal. If the school district is large enough to have a library media director or coordinator, decisions about accessing materials housed in the physical library collection are made centrally with campus input. Sometimes, however, the campus library media specialist will make these purchases, which require computer hardware and automation software, and peripherals such as a printer, a barcode scanner, and a hand-held portable inventory device. In the absence of district library media personnel, the campus librarian will need to consult with many library automation salespersons, colleagues in other districts, and possibly contact the State Library for consultation before making a decision about which system to purchase. These systems are expensive, but necessary.

Access to On-Shelf Materials and Subscription Databases

Also directly related to the librarian's responsibilities is the acquisition of online subscription databases to provide teachers and students with access to digital information sources for curricular and personal needs. These databases include articles from journals, magazines, newspapers, and encyclopedias. They also contain dictionaries, electronic books, audio and video files, and a variety of primary sources. This requires several workstation computers connected via a local area network (LAN) and to the Internet, allowing faculty and students to use the library's online catalog (usually housed on a file server in the building) to search for on-shelf materials such as books and DVDs and to use the Internet to access subscription databases. Students and teachers will need instruction in the use of these technologies so that they can access information and intellectually make meaning from it.

Schools now have a high-speed connection to the Internet and are posting Web pages for easy access to information about the school for parents, students, faculty and staff, and prospective families. Included in the school's Web site are pages specific to the library media center and its collection and services. It is on these pages that students can access their school's subscription databases and the library's catalog (if the Web version of the automation software is purchased), as well as a collection of curricular links on the free Web and original material created and posted by the library media specialist. As the information specialist, she (and not the school's or district's Web master) should create and maintain the library's Web presence.

Bibliographic Instruction

An additional responsibility of the library media specialist is teaching students how to find books and other materials. Because libraries have a standard organization of materials, the basic concept of library arrangement should transfer to most school and public libraries, and in general to university libraries, even though academic libraries usually implement a different classification system. When students are using the library for research, library media specialists will often integrate the skills into the information search process and teach it at point of need in the curriculum.

However, in order for students to access books for personal interest, there is often a need for the librarian to teach bibliographic skills (what one would think of as traditional "library skills") before they are needed for subject-area research. This process can begin with kindergarten students, allowing them to find for themselves books in the picture book (or Easy) section, progressing to showing them how to find books in that section by their favorite authors. This process takes time, and a creative library media specialist will develop engaging and meaningful activities to teach these skills. As students progress in cognitive ability, they can learn how fiction and nonfiction library materials are classified and shelved.

Students as young as second grade (and some first graders) can begin using the online catalog to perform simple subject and author searches (with help on spelling, as the catalog is generally unforgiving of spelling errors) and find books of personal interest on the shelf. The library media specialist will break this process into several developmentally appropriate steps, designing activities that effectively teach skills and allow for individual practice. Teaching shelf arrangement and use of the online catalog is a progressive and increasingly difficult set of skills taught and reinforced at each grade level. Middle and high school library media specialists continue bibliographic instruction, but many times this occurs with individuals rather than with whole classes.

Increasingly, students' needs become curricular based, involving information skills that are more sophisticated than learning to use the online catalog and the arrangement of the shelves. In these instances, whole-class instruction occurs during a collaborative unit that the library media specialist and teacher planned and are teaching together. This will begin as early as the primary grades and continue with each grade level. For further details on the effective teaching of information and communications technology skills, see the section

"Instructional Partnership" in this chapter and the section in chapter 2 on integrating the library media program across the school and curriculum.

Professional Productivity

A library media specialist uses technology for:

- Communicating with colleagues via e-mail or other digital communication tools

- Creating instructional materials for upcoming classes that he will teach, such as creating a project wiki that students will access for the task, resources, directions for showing results, and a self evaluation that also includes the scoring rubric

- Producing library newsletters and periodic updates for faculty

- Networking with library media specialists from around the state and country

- Developing the library's physical and online collections

- Answering students' and faculty's reference questions (e.g., "Who are the U.S. senators from North Carolina?" or "Our class needs to know how much rain Oregon had last year.")

- Taking online classes or training

- Keeping current on professional trends, issues, strategies, methodologies, and tools through social networks such as the Teacher-Librarian Ning or Twitter

- Reading news feeds from professional publications and blogs

- Updating a professional blog

- Reviewing new tools that allow students and teachers to produce, communicate, and participate with others online

- Researching Internet safety resources for students and teachers

- Searching for curriculum-related Internet resources

- Studying the online citation (bibliography) tools in order to choose the best for students to use

- Creating a Google Earth tour of a literary character's journey for students to use in their English or language class

- Creating original content for and maintaining the library's Web space

- Visiting Web sites of professional associations

Noninstructional Technology Duties

Unless the school has a technologist or technician whose main duties include acquiring, managing, and supporting technology in labs and classrooms, this responsibility often falls to the library media specialist. This practice varies widely across campuses and districts depending on the human resources available and the technical expertise of the library media specialist. The additional responsibility of maintaining computers in labs and classrooms may keep the library media specialist from important instructional interaction with students and teachers.

A library media specialist in an elementary school of 950 students, functioned by default as the instructional technologist. While her responsibilities were to include assisting teachers on the effective use of technology in the curriculum (in addition to technology as it related to information access), she found that much of her time was spent as a technician, troubleshooting broken computers and printers. She was unable to collaborate adequately with teachers or assist students in the information search process as required by the curriculum. The district administrators finally realized the job of managing all the technology on a large campus was overwhelming for one person and hired technologists (who often had the responsibility of more than one school) to support the labs and classrooms. This additional position gave her the opportunity to manage the library's technology resources and library programs, and allowed her time to collaborate with the technologist and classroom teachers for effective integration of information and communications technology skills into the curriculum.

In a small school, the library media specialist may be capable of managing all technology and helping teachers integrate it into their instruction. A knowledge of basic hardware configurations, trouble-shooting techniques, and available software programs is necessary for this level of support. In such a situation, the school should allow the library media specialist to seek appropriate training by providing funding and release time.

Audio and Photography Equipment

Often the purchase, maintenance, and inventory of equipment used to create, view, or listen to instructional materials and student products falls under the library media specialist's domain. Sometimes grade levels or departments will request purchases through the administration, but the maintenance and inventory may still lie within the scope of the library media program. Included are data projectors and computers; DVD players or VCRs for projection on large screens; digital scanners; digital video and still cameras; film editing equipment and software; overhead projectors; televisions; digital tape recorders; and CD players. The equipment may have a barcode affixed and its description entered into the library's database so that it can be checked out to a teacher or classroom, creating control over its whereabouts. When the equipment malfunctions, it is usually the librarian who is called to see to its repair. A library media specialist must assess whether the equipment should be repaired or retired. She should have a repair service to which she can send broken items.

Literacy Programmer

The third major role of the library media specialist is that of literacy programmer. Engaging students and faculty in the school library includes library media specialist-created programs that will entice them to use the library space and its collections. Typically these programs promote reading for pleasure, but often a program will integrate information process skills as well.

In elementary schools, typical programs may include:

- Story time
- Original reading incentive programs
- Promotion of the state book list (usually sponsored by the state's school library association or the educational media association)
- Guest authors and storytellers
- Guest readers or guest celebrity readers
- Book clubs
- Book fairs
- Author birthday celebrations
- Activities for Children's Book Week, National Library Week, and School Library Media Month, cultural and ethnic celebrations, Banned Books Week, National Library Card Sign Up Month, National Library Week, Women's History Month, Read Across America, President's Day, Public Schools Week, National Poetry Month, TV Turn-off Week, and other recognitions and holidays
- Activities to help public librarians promote the state or local summer reading programs

Elementary library media specialists will want to create an enticing and appealing atmosphere, which includes activities in which children and teachers will want to participate, and in which they will need library facilities and materials in order to do so. If time is a factor, the library media specialist can consider pairing two classes of the same or different grade levels to work collaboratively on projects.

Middle and high school libraries may include many of the aforementioned programs in addition to Teen Read Week, poetry slams, and writing contests such as "Letter to My Favorite Author." Getting teens into the library media center remains more of a challenge than promoting the programs to younger students, so library media specialists who serve older students will have to be creative. Using blogs to review new books, sponsoring online and electronic game tournaments, and having teens create podcasts that others can download to their personal music players brings teens to the virtual and physical library space. The American Library Association's divisions for school library media specialists (American Association of School Librarians and the Young Adult Library Services Association) have many programming ideas for children and teens. See the section on literacy in chapter 2 for additional ideas.

Reader Guidance

Connecting readers with quality literature is one of the most rewarding and beneficial tasks the literacy programmer undertakes. Making these connections requires a vast knowledge of authors and genre including fiction, nonfiction, and poetry titles on a range of reading levels. When a student or teacher approaches the library media specialist with a request to help him find a "good book," the librarian knows the appropriate questions to ask to connect that reader with the perfect title. She gets to know the interests of the students and teachers who often use the library collection for pleasure reading and seeks titles to meet their needs. Other ways a library media specialist connects students with good literature include book talks (presenting, live or digitally through a podcast, enough of a book's plot to entice a student to want to read it to find out how it ends), book reviews in the school newspaper or library newsletter or blog, book displays in the library and on the library's Web space, and book discussion groups.

Text Leveling: Another area where the library media specialist can assist teachers and students with literacy development is in the use of text leveling strategies to improve reading comprehension. In the hands of a well-trained professional like the library media specialist, such instructional techniques can greatly benefit students and help them to grasp concepts that might otherwise be inaccessible to them.

Text leveling protocols have been in use for some time; text leveling methods, such as Lexiles, are not a particularly new practice. However, one must be aware of the inappropriate uses or misapplications of this strategy to guard against potential unintended consequences:

- Text levels will shift, change and increase over time. A student's text level should not remain static. The use of text leveling must allow for ongoing assessment of a student's correct level in order for this intervention to be used appropriately and well. This is why it is critical that the library media specialist not be required to place a level in the student's record associated with the library's circulation system.

- Labeling books in the collection at a particular level and relegating students to only these selections limits their access to a variety of genres. Depending on the formula used to determine a book's level, some facets of the collection such as plays, poetry, and the works of particular writing styles may not be properly leveled and could be off limits to particular students.

- Associated with library book labeling is the potential stigma a student can experience when his or her access to the full collection is restricted. When a student may choose from only a limited portion of what the library has to offer this does little to promote enthusiastic, long-term library use or nurture a life-long love of reading.

Encouraging reluctant readers to read for pleasure remains a challenging task for both elementary and secondary librarians. Young children have many outside influences that deflect their attention from reading. Teens often have too much homework, a busy social life, prefer watching TV or chatting with friends on the phone or online, or have a part-time job that keeps them from reading for the pure enjoyment of it. Knowledgeable librarians develop the parts of the collection based on the interests of those students, and creative librarians use innovative methods to draw the reluctant readers into the library to see displays of books and magazines and hear about topics they enjoy.

Collection Developer

The fourth major role the library media specialist assumes is that of collection developer. The library media specialist partners with teachers to develop the library's collections by evaluating and purchasing quality literature and instructional materials to support curriculum standards and the demographic makeup of the school and community. "By being conversant with new research about reading, the school library media specialist can build a collection that reflects the needs of learners from a variety of backgrounds and cultures, and with diverse abilities and aspirations" (American Association of School Librarians 18). In following the spirit of intellectual freedom, the collection will provide students with a wide range of viewpoints on current and historical topics. This important task is best conducted in collaboration with teachers and students and consists of having a deep knowledge of both the curriculum and student interests. The library media specialist is knowledgeable about review sources, publisher catalogs, and collection development services (often a service provided by a publisher's salesperson or a book jobber, a company that fills orders for a library from many publishers). The librarian is responsible for knowing the scope of literature for the audience and the curriculum, popular and upcoming authors of fiction, and authoritative authors and publishers for nonfiction resources. In other words, she must have extensive knowledge of print and online resources and of her patrons and curriculum.

She purchases books, magazines, newspapers, subscription databases and electronic books, and DVDs and audio books for the library media center. These titles support the curriculum and student interests. The librarian surveys faculty and students for titles of interest and studies the curriculum for each subject and grade level to fill in gaps in the existing collection. She reads professional reviews and summaries to find the best titles to meet needs. Award-winning books such as Caldecott, Newbery, and Coretta Scott King (American Library Association) are included so students have access to the best titles available.

Developing a Culturally Responsive Collection

Leaders who strive for social justice and culturally responsive practices create and maintain instructional settings that promote equitable student outcomes for all learners (Robins, Lindsey, Lindsey, and Terrell 6). In the principal's instructional leadership role, this commitment to cultural proficiency extends to the library media center and the services of the library program. Because a students' culture is a pathway for learning (Tatum 29), the library collection should strongly reflect the history, language, rituals, and lifestyles of students in the school community. Students are eager to read and interact with texts that support and represent their multilingual, multicultural, or multifaceted identities. For these reasons, the library media specialist should be strongly supported as a collection developer who seeks out new, up-to-date volumes reflecting students' needs, cultures, languages, and interests.

For African American students, this means ready access to a wide array of culturally relevant fiction and nonfiction selections. "African American literature can help students understand history, substantiate their existence, and critically examine the present, as well as anticipate the political, social, and cultural changes that may affect students' lives" (Tatum 30). Purchasing award-winning books from lists such as the Tomás Rivera Mexican American Children's Book Award, honoring authors and literature depicting the Mexican American experience, can enhance the collection and allow students to read about characters who epitomize the legacy of their own families.

Materials Selection Policy

The library media specialist purchases titles that support various viewpoints on issues in accordance with the school district's Materials Selection Policy, which must usually have approval from the school's Board of Trustees. This policy may contain an opening statement about intellectual freedom and the student's right to read. It states the objectives of the collection including, but not limited to, provisions made for supporting the curriculum, including the varied interests and abilities of students; materials that represent a range of viewpoints and ethnic perspectives; and resources for developing citizens who practice critical analysis and make informed, intelligent decisions for success in their daily lives. The policy will include selection criteria for the learning resources, a paragraph on how gift materials will be treated, and a procedure for the reconsideration of materials.

Addressing Challenges to Books and Materials

Principals should be knowledgeable about the process *if* and, more realistically, *when* the ideas in materials, learning resources, and books are challenged on a campus. In most cases, the principal is the point person in handling protests or concerns about books and teaching materials. To assist campus staff in addressing such situations, a well-crafted, thorough district policy should be in place so that there is no doubt about the process, timelines, or related paper work.

A set of guiding beliefs, such as the following list of sample items, can aid school staff when designing policies and processes regarding material challenges.

1. Any district patron or employee can object to the use of a learning resource.

2. No one patron, employee, or family, however, should dictate what belongs in the library collection or what materials will be used for instruction.

3. While books or materials are under reconsideration, it is important they remain in circulation so that others have access to their ideas and information.

4. Challenged materials should not be removed from circulation based only on the ideas or themes expressed in them.

5. Faculty and staff members should be made fully aware of the policy through an annual review.

When a parent or district employee lodges a complaint about a particular book, the first step should be to have a face-to-face discussion with the individual about the concern. This gives the principal an opportunity to learn why the parent is troubled and what expectation they may have for action. While some parents are understandably concerned about what *their* child is reading, others may want to shape the reading material of the entire school or district. This, of course, is inappropriate, as noted in the preceding belief statements, and is exactly the reason well-defined challenge processes and policies are crucial.

Teachers, parent representatives, the librarian, and the principal constitute the typical materials or book reconsideration committee. It is imperative that specific timelines and an appeals protocol be described in the policy. Likewise, forms and attachments needed to make the process operate should be crafted and included as part of the policy. These forms can be made available online or in hard copy in the school or library office.

A Web search for "instructional materials selection policy" returns several dozen excellent examples of these policies. See the "Additional Resources" section at the end of this chapter for links to sample policies.

Program Administrator

A fifth role of the school library media specialist is that of program administrator (American Association of School Librarians 18). While the responsibilities of this role support the program, they do not always interact with teachers and students and may indirectly support curriculum. However, these responsibilities are important in keeping the library and its resources available to students and faculty. A wise principal understands the steps involved in the main responsibilities of the school library's program administrator.

Maintaining the Collection

Maintenance of the collection includes processing the books and other materials for placement on the library shelves, repairing damaged or worn books, ordering replacements for lost and stolen items, and removing dated or damaged titles. Weeding, or removal, of dated books and audiovisual materials is critical in maintaining a collection to meet the intellectual needs of students and faculty. Dated materials may give students inaccurate, racist, or sexist information. The library media specialist should weed the collection regularly and systematically, disposing of books so that none finds its way back into the library or a classroom collection. With training and supervision from the library media specialist, a library clerk or volunteer can assume most aspects of collection maintenance.

Providing Access to Materials through the Library's Online Catalog and Circulation System

Making books and other materials ready for access by students and faculty is one of the behind-the-scenes responsibilities of the library media specialist. School principals who have an understanding of these time-consuming, multistep procedures will be able to support the library media specialist by providing adequate funding and resources for this important task. The following summary can serve as a resource for principals who need to support a new librarian or one who is not professionally trained in the process of providing access to materials.

Cataloging provides physical and intellectual access to all library materials. Classification is one component of cataloging that categorizes materials into subjects through a controlled vocabulary. Standard circulation procedures allow the student or teacher to leave the library with the desired book, DVD, or other material. This combined practice standardizes access to the collection so users have the same access in any school, public, or academic library they use. If the library's physical collection (and increasingly, digital collections are being cataloged for easier access) is not cataloged in a central location in the district, or if the library media specialist cannot purchase the individual records to add the book's or DVD's information to the online catalog, then she must adhere to a strict standard when creating original catalog records. The tedious multistep process to providing access to materials in the physical (and online) collection takes an inordinate amount of time. For a more detailed account of cataloging, classification, and circulation options and procedures, see Appendix C.

Library Volunteer Program

In times of decreased budgets and increased student populations, school libraries are increasingly dependent on volunteers to help with clerical duties such as processing or shelving books and assisting at the circulation desk. Volunteers can help with the record keeping involved in reading incentive programs, make displays and bulletin boards, and prepare materials for the librarian to use in instruction. Occasionally, parent volunteers read to groups of young children and help them find books of interest. Volunteers may also work with English-language learners by conversing with them in their native languages or helping them to practice their English.

Developing a volunteer program falls under the responsibilities of the library media specialist. Often a well-organized parent association will include the library on the list of volunteer opportunities, assigning a co-ordinator to work with others in the library. However, most library media specialists must recruit and coordinate their volunteers. Some choose not to have these helpers in the library but would rather do the work themselves or with the assistance of the paraprofessional. However, there are not too many librarians who will turn down the offer of free help.

Once parent and community helpers are recruited, the next step is training and organizing them for assisting in the library. In addition to training volunteers to reshelve books and use the library's circulation software, instruction may also include issues such as confidentiality of student library records, working cooperatively with teachers and staff, and managing student behavior.

Volunteers can assume many important duties for the library media specialist and paraprofessional. They can fill in at the circulation desk, if the librarian or paraprofessional has to be out of the library for non-related duties or lunch breaks. Even though the circulation is automated, the desk must be supervised to make sure students actually check out their books or to provide help if needed, especially with younger children. When the library media specialist has volunteers assisting with clerical duties, she is freed to plan with teachers, teach classes, help students and teachers, read to classes, work on collection development, or any number of important tasks. The volunteer can also assist the paraprofessional with clerical duties, or in the absence of a parapro-fessional, accomplish these tasks herself under the supervision of the library media specialist. Students can also be recruited and trained for help in the library; however, they must have adult supervision.

Free labor should come with rewards. Periodically the library media specialist should acknowledge volunteers with small gifts or recognition in the parent association newsletter or on a bulletin board. Library volunteers might have checkout privileges with the same circu-lation period as the students. At least once a year, volunteers should be honored in some way. Many schools acknowledge all volunteers at the same time with a tea, reception, or appreciation celebration. However, one librarian also honored her volunteers each year with a homemade luncheon prepared by the library staff (all two of them). This included tablecloths and cloth napkins, a short talk containing funny anecdotes that had happened throughout the year and specific examples of how each volunteer's help had made a difference in the library media program, and a small gift, such as a picture frame or lapel pin. She also prepared individualized bookplates stating, "This book is placed in the (name of school) Library Media Center in honor of volunteer (name of volunteer) for her hours of dedication to our young readers," followed by the date. Each recipient chose from a number of new books, one in which to have the bookplate affixed. The principal attended the luncheon and also thanked the group for their service to students. While going to this extent may not be necessary, each year the volunteers must be recognized and thanked in some special way.

Communicating with Public Libraries That Serve the School's Attendance Area

The public library is critical to meeting the needs of all students. School libraries rarely have the resources to stay open on school nights or weekends; so many students rely on a public library for academic and personal needs. If the library media specialist and the public librarian serving youth communicate, students will have a wider range of resources and assistance from two or more dynamic, knowledgeable professionals. The school librarian can indirectly help students and assist the public librarian in a number of ways:

1. Survey teachers, grade levels, or departments to find out when major assignments or projects are due throughout the year and communicate the topics and dates to the public librarians. The public librarians will be able to prepare for the onslaught of students and possibly put materials on reserve before the rush.

2. Talk to the children's or youth librarian about the information search process the school uses to give her a common vocabulary to use with students.

3. Borrow materials from the public library to keep on reserve in the school library for those research units for which there are inadequate resources.

4. Help the public librarian promote summer reading programs.

5. Encourage students to get a public library card and use those facilities after school and on weekends. Talk about the collection and

electronic databases available at the public library that will support their assignments.

Focusing on Priorities

As noted in this chapter, the most important roles of the library media specialist include that of instructional partner, information specialist, literacy programmer, and collection developer. There are many additional responsibilities the librarian assumes under the role of program administrator to ensure that the library media program runs efficiently and the school community is effectively using library and information resources. However, it is in the administrative details that a library media specialist can spend many hours a day, instead of with the more important roles that can increase student learning and achievement. When the librarian is required to use instructional time to manage a commercial electronic reading program, take school furniture and textbook inventory, or troubleshoot technology hardware problems, opportunities for meaningful student learning are missed. To increase student achievement, the library media specialist will spend more time on collaborating with teachers to integrate information and communications technology skills into the subject area curriculum and less time on administrative tasks. The continuum in Figure 3.1 can be used to assess how the library media specialist spends her time and how steps can be taken to ensure that she is spending more time on instructional and curriculum-related tasks and less on administrative functions.

Essential Concepts for This Chapter

The library media specialist's unique and important roles and responsibilities contribute to the achievement of students and the success of teachers. They provide faculty with a partner who collaborates with them for quality instruction and gives teachers and students access to the best materials and technology for teaching and learning. An excellent library media program is the result of the principal's support and the library media specialist's dedication to these tasks.

Planning for Action and Getting Started

1. Become familiar with the state and national standards for a quality library media program and discuss these standards with the library media specialist, as related to her roles and responsibilities.

2. Compare instructional roles to noninstructional duties of the library media specialist to gauge whether or not time is prioritized in favor of meaningful student learning.

(Examples of Instructional/Curricular Tasks)	(Examples of Noninstructional Tasks)
Instructional Partner ☐ Collaborating with teachers to plan and deliver instruction to students ☐ Teaching integrated information and communications technology (ICT) skills ☐ Assessing ICT skills **Information Specialist** ☐ Using technology tools and resources to engage students with ideas and information ☐ Introducing effective new technologies to faculty and students ☐ Connecting students and faculty to a global learning community ☐ Promoting ethical use of ideas and information ☐ Extending instructional services beyond the classroom and library walls and hours ☐ Designing and developing curriculum **Literacy Programmer** ☐ Developing a vast knowledge of authors and genres ☐ Creating original reading incentive programs ☐ Connecting individual students with the right book ☐ Hosting guest authors and storytellers ☐ Promoting state book lists ☐ Encouraging students to read award-winning books ☐ Conducting live and digital book talks ☐ Encouraging reluctant readers to read for pleasure **Collection Developer** ☐ Developing a culturally responsive collection ☐ Collaborating with teachers and students to select appropriate resources ☐ Evaluating and purchasing quality on-shelf and online resources supporting various viewpoints	**Program Administrator** ☐ Providing staff development for faculty ☐ Acquiring and managing technology hardware, such as digital video recorders and cameras ☐ Keeping current on emerging technologies ☐ Providing physical access to materials ☐ Orienting students and faculty to the library media program and facilities ☐ Developing and maintaining a volunteer program ☐ Gathering materials and online resources ☐ Maintaining the library's Web site ☐ Creating lists of on-shelf and online resources for specific subjects and topics ☐ Creating and maintaining a budget ☐ Promoting safe and ethical Internet use ☐ Analyzing data and reporting statistics ☐ Communicating with public libraries ☐ Setting goals ☐ Maintaining membership in professional organizations ☐ Reading professional literature in and out of the school library field **Program Administrator** (continued) ☐ Managing commercial electronic reading incentive programs ☐ Collecting fines ☐ Ordering supplies ☐ Repairing damaged materials ☐ Reshelving books ☐ Trouble-shooting technology such as repairing computers and printers and replacing cartridges **Non-library-related tasks** ☐ Issuing student identification cards ☐ Maintaining the campus inventory ☐ Managing textbook distribution and collection ☐ Covering classes for absent faculty ☐ Proctoring tests ☐ Monitoring students in the cafeteria

Figure 3.1. Quality Continuum of Instructional Time for Library Media Specialists

3. If one does not exist, create a job description in collaboration with the library media specialist.

4. Refer to *Empowering Learners: Guidelines for School Library Media Programs* for additional information on the responsibilities of the position. If you are in a large district, ask the library coordinator or other principals for assistance. Revisit the library media specialist's job description each year to make modifications or additions as necessary.

5. Discuss the responsibilities with the library media specialist. There are a finite number of hours in a day, so the expectations should be manageable. Consider the amount of clerical help available when assigning extra duties.

6. Find out whether your school district has a selection and reconsideration policy and become familiar and comfortable with it. If your school or district does not have such a policy, strongly encourage decision makers to develop and adopt one.

7. Encourage the library media specialist to recruit volunteers if none currently assist in the library.

8. Ask teachers to give the library media specialist a list of major assignments and projects so that she can share those with the public librarians who serve the school's attendance area.

9. In collaboration with the library media specialist, promote the public library to students as an extension of their school library media center and encourage students to obtain a library card.

Works Cited

American Association of School Librarians. *Empowering Learners: Guidelines for School Library Media Programs*. Chicago: American Library Association, 2009.

Robins, Kikanza Nuri, Randall B. Lindsey, Delores B. Lindsey, and Raymond D. Terrell. *Culturally Proficient Instruction: A Guide for People Who Teach*. Thousand Oaks, CA: Corwin Press, 2002.

Tatum, Alfred W. "Nesting Grounds." *Principal Leadership* 2.2 (2001): 26–32.

Additional Resources
Instructional Partner

Buzzeo, Toni. *Collaborating to Meet Standards: Teacher/Librarian Partnerships for K-2*. Columbus, OH: Linworth Publishing, 2007.

Buzzeo, Toni. *Collaborating to Meet Standards: Teacher/Librarian Partnerships for K-6*. 2nd ed. Columbus, OH: Linworth Publishing, 2007.

Buzzeo, Toni. *Collaborating to Meet Standards: Teacher/Librarian Partnerships for 7–12*. Worthington, OH: Linworth Publishing, 2002.

Buzzeo, Toni. *The Collaboration Handbook*. Columbus, OH: Linworth Publishing, 2008.

Harada, Violet H., and Hoan M. Yoshina. *Assessing Learning: Librarians and Teachers as Partners*. Westport, CT: Libraries Unlimited, 2005.

Harada, Violet H., Carolyn H. Kirio, and Sandra H. Yamamoto. *Collaborating for Project-Based Learning for Grades 9–12*. Columbus, OH: Linworth Publishing, 2008.

Harada, Violet H., and Joan M. Yoshina. *Inquiry Learning through Librarian-Teacher Partnerships*. Worthington, OH: Linworth Publishing, 2004.

Harker, Christa, and Dorette Putonti. *Library Research with Emergent Readers: Meeting Standards through Collaboration*. Columbus, OH: Linworth Publishing, 2008.

Moreillon, Judi. *Collaborative Strategies for Teaching Reading Comprehension: Maximizing Your Impact*. Chicago: American Library Association, 2007.

Volkman, John D. *Collaborative Library Research Projects: Inquiry That Stimulates the Senses*. Westport, CT: Libraries Unlimited, 2008.

Information Specialist

Bell, Ann. *Handheld Computers in Schools and Media Centers*. Columbus, OH: Linworth Publishing, 2007.

Braun, Linda W. *Technology Tools for the Busy Teen Librarian: Making Teen Services Work*. Westport, CT: Libraries Unlimited, 2009.

Church, Audrey P. *Your Library Goes Virtual*. Columbus, OH: Linworth Publishing, 2007.

Conover, Patricia Ross. *Technology Projects for Library Media Specialists and Teachers*. Columbus, OH: Linworth Publishing, 2007.

Cuban, Sandra, and Larry Cuban. *Partners in Literacy: Schools and Libraries Building Communities through Technology*. Chicago: American Library Association, 2007.

Davidson, Susanna, and Everyl Yankee. *Web Site Design with the Patron in Mind: A Step-by-Step Guide for Libraries*. Chicago: American Library Association, 2003.

Farmer, Lesley S. J. *Teen Girls and Technology: What's the Problem, What's the Solution?* Chicago: American Library Association, 2008.

Leckie, Gloria J., and John E. Buschman, eds. *Information Technology in Librarianship*. Westport, CT: Libraries Unlimited, 2008.

Neiburger, Eli. *Gamers . . . in the Library? The Why, What, and How of Videogame Tournaments for All Ages*. Chicago: American Library Association, 2007.

Zmuda, Allison, and Violet H. Harada. *Librarians as Learning Specialists: Meeting the Learning Imperative for the 21st Century*. Westport, CT: Libraries Unlimited, 2008.

Literacy Programmer

Collins, Joan. *Motivating Readers in the Middle Grades*. Columbus, OH: Linworth Publishing, 2008.

Diamont-Cohen, Betsy, and Selma K. Levi. *Booktalking Bonanza: Ten Ready-to-Use Multimedia Sessions for the Busy Librarian*. Chicago: American Library Association, 2009.

Hinton, KaaVonia, and Gail K. Dickinson. *Integrating Multicultural Literature in Libraries and Classrooms in Secondary Schools*. Columbus, OH: Linworth Publishing, 2007.

Knowles, Elizabeth, and Martha Smith. *Boys and Literacy: Practical Strategies for Librarians, Teachers, and Parents*. Englewood, CO: Libraries Unlimited, 2005.

Knowles, Elizabeth, and Martha Smith. *Reading Rules!: Motivating Teens to Read*. Englewood, CO: Libraries Unlimited, 2001.

Miller, Pat. *Reaching Every Reader: Instructional Strategies in the Library for Grades K–5*. 2nd ed. Columbus, OH: Linworth Publishing, 2008.

Ray, Virginia Lawrence. *School Wide Book Events: How to Make Them Happen*. Englewood, CO: Libraries Unlimited, 2003.

Reid Rob. *Reid's Read-Alouds: Selections for Children and Teens*. Chicago: American Library Association, 2009.

Sullivan, Michael. *Connecting Boys with Books 2: Closing the Reading Gap*. Chicago: American Library Association, 2009.

Collection Developer

Barr, Catherine, and John T. Gillespie. *Best Books for High School Readers, Grades 9–12*. 2nd ed. Westport, CT: Libraries Unlimited, 2009.

Barr, Catherine, and John T. Gillespie. *Best Books for Middle School and Junior High Readers, Grades 6–9*. 2nd ed. Westport, CT: Libraries Unlimited, 2009.

Bishop, Kay. *The Collection Program in Schools: Concepts, Practices, and Information Sources*. Westport, CT: Libraries Unlimited, 2007.

Brenner, Robin E. *Understanding Manga and Anime*. Westport, CT: Libraries Unlimited, 2007.

Drew, Bernard A. *100 Most Popular African American Authors: Biographical Sketches and Bibliographies*. Westport, CT: Libraries Unlimited, 2006.

Hubbard, Benjamin J., John T. Hatfield, and James A. Santucci. *An Educator's Guide to America's Religious Beliefs and Practices*. Westport, CT: Libraries Unlimited, 2007.

Intner, Sheila S., and Jean Weihs. *Standard Cataloging for School and Public Libraries*. Westport, CT: Libraries Unlimited, 2007.

Kaplan, Allison G., and Ann Marlow Riedling. *Catalog It! A Guide to Cataloging School Library Materials*. 2nd ed. Columbus, OH: Linworth Publishing, 2006.

Knowles, Elizabeth, and Martha Smith. *Understanding Diversity through Novels and Picture Books*. Westport, CT: Libraries Unlimited, 2007.

Kravitz, Nancy. *Censorship and the School Library Media Center*. Englewood, CO: Libraries Unlimited, 2002.

Luckenbill, W. Bernard. *Collection Development for a New Century in the School Library Media Center*. Englewood, CO: Libraries Unlimited, 2002.

Martinez, Sara E. *Latino Literature: A Guide to Reading Interests*. Westport, CT: Libraries Unlimited, 2008.

Olson, Nancy B. *Cataloging of Audiovisual Materials and Other Special Materials*. Westport, CT: Libraries Unlimited, 2008.

Slote, Stanley J. *Weeding Library Collections: Library Weeding Methods*. 4th ed. Englewood, CO: Libraries Unlimited, 1997.

Webber, Carlisle K. *Gay, Lesbian, Bisexual, Transgender and Questioning Teen Literature: A Genre Guide*. Westport, CT: Libraries Unlimited, 2008.

Wilk, Joseph J. *Inclusive Library Services for Lesbian, Gay, Bisexual, Transgender, and Queer/Questioning Teens*. Westport, CT: Libraries Unlimited, 2009.

Challenges to Books and Materials

American Library Association. "Challenged Materials: An Interpretation of the Library Bill of Rights." 28 Jan. 2009. <http://www.ala.org/ala/aboutala/offices/oif/statementspols/statementsif/interpretations/challengedmaterials.cfm>.

American Library Association. "Workbook for Selection Policy Writing." 1998. <http://www.ala.org/Template.cfm?Section=dealing&Template=/ContentManagement/ContentDisplay.cfm&ContentID=11173>.

Program Administrator

Baule, Steven M. *Facilities Planning for School Library Media and Technology Centers*. 2nd ed. Columbus, OH: Linworth Publishing, 2007.

Lankford, Mary. *Leadership and the School Librarian*. Columbus, OH: Linworth Publishing, 2006.

Morris, Betty J. *Administering the School Library Media Center*. 4th ed. Englewood, CO: Libraries Unlimited, 2004.
> Includes not only administrative roles, but also addresses those of instructional partnership.

Repman, Judi, and Gail K. Dickinson, eds. *School Library Management*. 6th ed. Columbus, OH: Linworth Publishing, 2007.

Rosenfield, Ester, and David V. Loertscher, eds. *Toward a 21st-Century School Library Media Program*. Lanham, MD: The Scarecrow Press, 2007.
> Addresses most areas of school librarianship, including 21st-century skills, new technology tools, literacy, and instructional partnership.

Schultz-Jones, Barbara. *An Automation Primer for School Library Media Centers*. Columbus, OH: Linworth Publishing, 2006.

Stephens, Claire Gatrell, and Patricia Franklin. *Library 101: A Handbook for the School Library Media Specialist*. Westport, CT: Libraries Unlimited, 2007.

Toor, Ruth, and Hilda K. Weisburg. *New on the Job: A School Library Media Specialist's Guide to Success*. Chicago: American Library Association, 2007.

Woolls, Blanche. *The School Library Media Manager*. 4th ed. Westport, CT: Libraries Unlimited, 2008.
> Includes most administrative roles of the library media specialist, including issues such as Internet filtering, the USA Patriot Act, certification and national guidelines, and impact of new technologies.

Ziarnik, Natalie Reif. *School and Public Libraries: Developing the Natural Alliance*. Chicago: American Library Association, 2002.

CHAPTER 4

The Principal's Role in Supporting and Sustaining the Library Media Program

GUIDING QUESTIONS

What should a principal know about hiring and appraising the library media staff?

What critical factors should be considered when budgeting and scheduling for the library media program?

How should library media facilities be organized and utilized?

How can the principal serve as an advocate for the library program?

Introduction

Administrators matter! Principals oversee the educational and organizational well-being of the campus and manage the infrastructure for teaching and learning success. "As the instructional leader of the school and key person in providing a framework and climate for implementing the curriculum, the principal should acknowledge the importance of an effective school library service and encourage the use of it" (International Federation of Library Associations/UNESCO 15). This chapter guides campus leaders in performing specific administrative tasks essential to developing and sustaining successful library media programs, such as recruiting, hiring, and appraising personnel, planning for and managing funds, designing the schedule, allocating learning space, and developing relationships with those outside the school as advocates for strong libraries.

Staffing the Library Media Program and Hiring a Library Media Specialist

Just as the principal plays a critical role in selecting, supporting, and appraising general teaching faculty, she must do the same with library media center faculty. Effective library media specialists have many of the same characteristics as a fine teacher—they are energetic, patient, creative, intelligent, well read, cheerful, altruistic, and service oriented. The American Association of School Librarians guideline on staffing states that, "All students, teachers, and administrators in each school building at all grade levels must have access to a library media program provided by one or more certificated library media specialists working full-time in the school's library media center" (American Association of School Librarians, "Position Statement on Appropriate Staffing for School Library Media Centers").

The main roles of the professional library media specialist include collaborating with teachers in selecting materials for instruction and in teaching information and communications technology (ICT) skills to foster life-long learners, working well with children or teens, promoting literature to nurture avid readers, and developing book and digital resource collections to support curriculum and the interests of children or teens. According to findings of a study examining library media services and student achievement in the state of Colorado, there is a positive relationship between adequate professional staffing and higher academic performance on reading assessments (Lance, Rodney, and Hamilton-Pennell 39). See chapter 1 for more information.

When a school has the opportunity to hire a librarian, it is a vital task, requiring a team approach and serious and thoughtful consideration. A list of potential candidates can be selected after screening applications for those who hold a master's degree in library and information science from an American Library Association-accredited program and library media certification. Be cautious when considering for a position an individual who does not hold a degree in the library field. In some states and regions of the country, those seeking a library post can sit for an examination without participating in a graduate program. This creates a situation in which the potential library media specialist may lack the core body of knowledge, theories, philosophies, and credibility necessary to effectively develop and maintain a collection and collaborate with teachers to provide effective instruction for students. (For more recruiting ideas, see AASL's Web site, available at http://www.ala.org/aasl.)

If a candidate holding a masters degree and certification is not available, be mindful that the individual hired will require additional assistance through professional learning and sustained support. Increasingly, high-quality master's degree programs are available online and may be a viable alternative for those in remote sites or without direct access to universities or certification programs. Additional learning options are on-site training or mentoring activities with an experienced, certified librarian.

After a slate of candidates has been identified, a group composed of teachers, administrators, and members of the campus advisory or site council (including parents and students, when appropriate) should assemble to conduct interviews for the library media position. Prior to holding interviews, the team should meet to discuss the library media program, the role of the library media specialist in the school, and the philosophies and beliefs held by teachers and administrators about library media services. They should also talk about questions they plan to ask and make decisions concerning what kinds of responses they hope to hear from potential candidates. Following is a sample set of questions. Depending on the time available for each interview, team members could ask 8–10 questions, selecting those most suitable for the library program needs. See Appendix D for a worksheet to use during the interview.

QUESTIONS FOR INTERVIEWING A LIBRARY MEDIA SPECIALIST

- Briefly describe your view of the role of a library media specialist as a member of a professional learning community.

- What kinds of collaborations are appropriate for librarians and teachers?

- Define the term "flexible scheduling" as it applies to the library and tell how you would convince a teacher who did not want to do flexible scheduling to embrace it.

- A teacher wants to schedule her class to visit the library at the same time once a week for a library lesson and book exchange. How will you convince her to allow her students to exchange books several times per week and plan with you for instruction as needed in her curriculum?

- How do you stay current on emerging technologies, especially as they apply to the library media program?

- How do you see emerging technologies supporting instruction and what role does the library media specialist play in integrating these tools?

- How do you decide what information and communications technology skills to teach to students and when they should be taught in the curriculum?

- Describe the role of the library paraprofessional.

- How would you publicize a special library activity?

- Tell us about a recent professional/staff development activity you found beneficial.

- How would you use parent/community volunteers and student assistants to support your campus library program?

- What experience have you had in building a school library budget?

- A parent wishes to donate to the library a book that obviously supports a particular religious belief. What would you do?

- Explain why it is important for a school district to have an instructional materials book selection policy.

- Define a culturally responsive collection. How would you go about developing one for our school?

- A teacher requests that you duplicate a DVD from the local video store. What would you do?

- How will you educate teachers and students about ethical issues such as copyright and intellectual property?

- If we were able to talk to the students you have worked with, what would they tell us about you?

- As a librarian, to what professional organizations do you belong?

(These questions were adapted from a list originally created by Carlyn Gray, Director of Library Media Services in the Round Rock Independent School District, Round Rock, Texas.)

Hiring a Paraprofessional

Effective library media program facilitators recognize the importance of qualified clerical or paraprofessional assistance. Based on the size of the school and levels served, libraries should have one (or more) library aides to assist the professionals on staff with a wide range of responsibilities and activities, such as:

- Assisting with book selection and checkout
- Assisting with student use of the online catalog and reference databases
- Processing new books and materials for use
- Running circulation reports and overdue notices
- Shelving books and materials
- Creating book displays
- Checking in books and materials from students and teachers
- Maintaining printers and other items related to library media center technology
- Assisting with and supervising parent and student volunteers
- Keeping the library media center orderly and ready for use
- Repairing books and materials and cleaning equipment
- Supervising students
- Working with teachers and classes of students under the supervision of the library media specialist
- Generally assisting the library media specialist, as needed

Candidates for a library aide's position should have a high school diploma. When available, university or college students or those studying in a School of Library and Information Science program make superb candidates for such positions. Retired professionals also make excellent choices as library aides. After screening applicants, the librarian and principal should conduct an interview. See Appendix E for a worksheet to use during the interview. Consider posing some of the following questions.

- Please describe your organizational skills and strengths.
- What experience do you have working with children?
- Suppose you are assisting several students who need to check out their library books when a teacher sends a student to the library media center with a request for assistance. What would you do?
- Tell us about your experience working with others in a collaborative setting.

- How would you approach and work with a group of noisy students in the library media center?

- A student in your school has a book out that is now six weeks overdue and wants to check out another book. How would you handle this situation?

- You're helping a student with the online catalog and the phone keeps ringing. What do you do?

- Describe your proficiency with technology tools.

Once the paraprofessional or aide is hired, he should work with the library media specialist to establish a schedule and list of duties to help the library media center and its team function productively. While it is understandable that on occasion the paraprofessional's assistance may be required outside the library, taking him away from his scheduled duties in the library may keep the library media specialist from working instructionally with teachers and students. When the paraprofessional is not on duty in the library, the professional must accomplish the clerical duties needed to keep the library functioning.

Appraising the Library Media Staff

In addition to helping teachers and others improve their practice through professional growth and supervision (see GEAR Method improvement tool in chapter 5), principals have the important responsibility of appraising staff performance on a yearly or biyearly basis for the purpose of contract extension or renewal. Because the library media specialist is a teacher, his performance should be appraised with the same state, district, or campus-adopted instrument and process used with the general teaching faculty. Because of the unique nature of the position, however, the principal must also assess additional responsibilities assumed by the library media specialist with a form or instrument targeting specific domains affiliated with librarianship.

At a preobservation conference, the principal and library media specialist can discuss expectations for the appraisal experience. This may require reviewing the job description as well as any additional standards for performance that may be applicable. These will include, for instance, collaboration with teachers, integration of information and communications technology skills with subject area curricula, collection development, cataloging, and administrative responsibilities, including supervision of paraprofessionals. At this conference it would also be appropriate to discuss the means of data and information gathering for the process such as in-class observations, planning and scheduling records, and other documents associated with library media-related services.

In many schools and districts, the principal is also expected to appraise all paraprofessional staff. This task, for the library media program, should be conducted in collaboration with the librarian and based on the general duties assigned to the paraprofessional. This is a time to celebrate recognized strengths of the paraprofessional as well as be very clear about expectations for improved performance.

Budgeting for the Library Media Program

The annual operating budget is the fiscal representation of a school's goals and initiatives. When campus leaders and decision makers allocate dollars to grade levels, departments, and various programs across the school, the library media program should be considered as well, because it serves every student and teacher. Each year the library media specialist should come to the budget-planning table to present funding needs, explain budget requests, and advocate for a share of available resources. A well-informed administrative team will use this data to assist them in making budgeting decisions. It is critical to note that, "the size of school library's staff and collection is the best school predictor of academic achievement, and students who score higher on standardized tests tend to come from schools with more school library staff and more books, periodicals, and video materials regardless of other factors such as economic ones" (IFLA/UNESCO 7).

As the library media specialist develops the annual budget, she must take into consideration an array of funding requirements. These include the following items.

- Computer hardware and software
- General supplies
- Book repair supplies
- Books and periodicals
- Audio-visual equipment
- Online subscription databases
- Ebooks
- Video streaming such as Safari Montage or Discovery Streaming
- Audiobooks

- Bookbinding

- Equipment repairs and cleaning

- Support agreements for circulation/cataloging software or Web-based services

- Maintaining the on-site professional collection

- Conference registrations and travel

- Author and storyteller visits

- Promotional and special reading events

- Professional organization membership fees

A vital facet of collection development is *weeding the collection* each year to remove outdated materials and resources. Replacement materials should be purchased to keep the collection accurate and up-to-date. If schools are using print versions of an encyclopedia, for example, the set should be replaced every five to six years. Replacement and renewal needs are integral to the annual campus budget planning and allocation process.

At the district level, principals should work with decision makers to advocate for library funding in the district budget process. A yearly line item amount flowing directly from the central administrative budget to the campus librarian will guarantee that many vital needs will be addressed. It is imperative that these funds not be diverted to other programs or purposes on the campus. Appendixes F and G offer worksheets to help the librarian in the budgeting process.

Scheduling for an Effective Program

Central to managing the campus infrastructure is building and maintaining the school's master schedule. Instructional and programmatic needs must drive the schedule, not vice versa. It is essential for principals and other administrative decision makers to understand best practice associated with library media scheduling. The following information will help campus leaders make sound decisions about organizing the school day so that the library will function productively and effectively for both students and staff.

Library media programs can operate under one of two basic schedules: fixed or flexible. Because of organizational rigors and demands, an increasing number of elementary library programs are unfortunately moving to a rotational or *fixed schedule*, wherein the library media specialist teaches or reads to the same class and students exchange books, at the same time every week. Many elementary and most middle and high schools keep a *flexible schedule*, allowing students and teachers to use the library media center at point of need, integrating the library media center with grade-level content or curriculum.

Disadvantages of a Fixed Schedule

Elementary library programs often implement fixed schedules in order to give classroom teachers a conference or planning period each day. Classes may rotate each week through sessions with the library media specialist, along with art, music, and physical education teachers. Putting the library into the rotation prevents classroom teachers from helping individual children choose books appropriate for their interests and reading levels. They cannot help students make important connections between the library media program and the classroom.

This scheduling arrangement and philosophy also prevents and impedes access for classes that need to use the collection and library space and the expertise of the library media specialist. Students should be able to visit the library every day if needed. If a student checks out a book on Tuesday and decides that evening that it is not suitable, or she finishes it in two days, she should not have to wait until the following Tuesday to exchange it.

Effective practice dictates that the library media program *not* be included in the rotation in order to maintain a flexible schedule. Art, music, and physical education have stated, prescribed content objectives, but the library media curriculum consists mainly of information and communications technology skills. These are process skills that need to be integrated into their subject areas in order for students to effectively learn the skills in order to acquire the prescribed content.

Library media specialists working in fixed-schedule environments have limited flexible time for substantive collaboration with teachers or working meaningfully on administrative duties. Some library media specialists may choose to use the fixed model, preferring to have a predictable schedule with adequate time allowed for administrative tasks and occasional collaboration with teachers. The principal should discourage the librarian from keeping a fixed schedule so that she is able to teach at point of need and meet with teachers during their conference/planning times. Instead of putting the library media specialist and the library media center into the rotation with art, music, and physical education, allow the library media specialist to use her expertise in developing the library collection and collaborating with teachers to integrate process skills into the curriculum.

Advantages of a Fixed Schedule

To ensure that all students visit the library media specialist at least once a week, some professionals prefer a fixed schedule. Students and teachers can anticipate the visit, returning books and enjoying story time or bibliographic instruction on a regular basis. The library media specialist knows that all students have the same opportunities and that all classes are receiving equal instruction. The teacher and library media specialist should not, however, expect students to exchange books on one set day per week, but allow them to visit the library several times a week, if needed, to choose another book. *Just to be clear, we do not condone a fixed schedule in the elementary school, especially in the upper grades.* The impact that a flexible schedule has on student learning should outweigh the advantages of a fixed schedule.

Advantages of a Flexible Schedule

Effective practice allows students to visit the library as needed for book exchange or for integrated information and communications technology skills instruction. Flexible scheduling enables library media specialists and teachers to collaborate and schedule the library media center in order to integrate the state-prescribed content objectives with information and technology skills at point of need in the curriculum. Another way to think about it is scheduling by objective, which provides the most effective model for library media programs.

How Does Flexible Scheduling Work?

As a classroom teacher plans instruction to meet curriculum objectives, he and the library media specialist should work together to design instruction, which integrates curriculum standards with accompanying ICT skills. Often, the library media specialist teaches the information skills needed to access and use the information required to acquire the subject-area content knowledge. If the school has a technology teacher, planning and teaching can be a three-way collaboration, with the technology teacher teaching the technology skills used to communicate results. (In many states' curriculum standards, these skills are embedded in the content areas and do not stand alone in a library media curriculum.) The librarian's time is then scheduled for as many sessions as needed, at the time that is most convenient for the classroom teacher's schedule. By having a flexible schedule, the library media specialist and teacher can spend as many consecutive days as needed with a class to complete the project.

There will be weeks on the librarian's schedule that are very full, with most of each day devoted to teaching. On the other hand, there will be some weeks that may not have as much face-to-face instruction with classes. The library media specialist will use this time for collection and program development, planning with teachers for future instruction, and completing administrative and clerical duties.

Jean Donham van Deusen notes that there are five key elements in making flexible scheduling work:

- *Information skills curriculum matched with content area curriculum*
- *Flexible access*

  It is important to note that moving from a fixed to a flexible schedule should not mean that students have no access to the library simply because their classes do not have a regular time to visit each week. The library media specialist must ensure that all students have access and that she is planning with teachers on a regular basis to bring classes in for integrated information skills instruction. With flexible scheduling in place, the weekly visit to the library is no longer guaranteed. In order for children to become readers, to have guidance in selecting appropriate books, and to have access to reading materials, provisions must be made for students to have access to the collection. Having the library open to unscheduled visits by any student also requires the classroom teacher to accommodate those visits in his daily schedule. If a shortened schedule (15 minutes or so) is needed to maintain continuity, the teacher should attend with the class so he can assist in book selection, especially if the library media specialist is working with another class in integrated instruction.

- *Team planning*

  Research suggests that librarians can provide some leadership with grade-level or content-area teams as they plan together.

- *Principal expectations*

  In the 1994 study, *The Impact of Scheduling on Curriculum Consultation and Information Skills Instruction,* van Deusen and Tallman found that 'when principals had expectations for the librarian to participate in instructional planning with teachers, such participation occurred. The importance of principals sharing the vision of the library resource center program as a collaborative partner in classroom instruction cannot be overlooked' (20).

- *Commitment to resource-based learning*

  Library media specialists play an important role in:

  - Identifying digital and print resources and recommending ways in which those resources can be used in teaching and learning.

  - Resource-based learning, which facilitates a constructivist approach to learning; it facilitates student engagement and active learning.

  - Resource-based learning, which also provides the appropriate classroom structures to facilitate free flow to and from the library media center; children are engaged in active work, and the classroom tends not to be teacher centered. In such settings, movement to and from the library resource center, as needs arise, is natural. By working collaboratively with teachers to integrate a variety of resources into their teaching, the teacher/librarian acts as a catalyst for these approaches. If there is no commitment to resource-based learning, it is difficult to envision flexible scheduling serving much of a purpose; the teacher/librarian has less to offer in a textbook-bound approach to teaching. (van Deusen 17–18)

See "Collaboration" in chapter 2 for detailed information on teacher/ librarian collaboration.

Moving from Fixed to Flexible Scheduling

If the school needs a way to provide time for the teachers' conference/planning period, consider having parent volunteers or sup- port staff supervise a corner of the library or an open classroom so that classes can go into the facility and read silently for pleasure (Loertscher 72). In his book, *The Power of Reading*, Krashen's study shows that reading achievement increases when children read for pleasure from self-selected books. Check with the district's legal department or lawyer to make sure that volunteers can supervise students without an employee present. If not, use the story time area of the library while the library media specialist is working with classes in the instructional area. Volun- teers can also read aloud to classes from books relating to the curriculum or from special reading lists such as state reading awards programs. This practice would be more beneficial for the students and enable the library media specialist to use her time in a way that more effectively helps teachers and students.

By implementing a flexible schedule, teachers and their students will effectively use print and digital resources, and students will know how a school library can be used. When they move from the elementary school to a middle school and high school with an open-access schedule, they will be more likely to use library materials and services as a natural extension of their educational process.

Optimizing a Fixed Schedule

If there is no other alternative than keeping a fixed library schedule, consider ways that will offer some access to the library media center for teachers and students in addition to those who are scheduled. David Loertscher suggests that individuals and small groups have access to the library media center even though scheduled classes are in session (72). The facility should be arranged so this can occur. Classes can read silently with supervision from volunteers or staff, freeing the library media specialist to work with classes. Another alternative might be to schedule classes only once every two to three weeks so the librarian can work with teachers at point of need.

LIBRARY MEDIA CENTER FACILITIES

In her role as instructional leader, the principal makes critical decisions about the form and functionality of campus instructional spaces, including the school library. The instructional mission of the library media center should be represented in its furnishings and format. "The aesthetic appearance contributes to the feeling of welcome as well as the desire for the school community to spend time in the library" (IFLA/UNESCO 8). A warm and inviting atmosphere with natural and ample lighting, comfortable seating, generous open spaces, and sufficient storage areas is essential for a positive learning environment and productive working site.

The library media center is the instructional center of the campus. Does it promote an atmosphere that invites students and teachers to read, learn, and collaborate in the facility? Take a look around. The best way to determine this is to take a walking tour of the facility with the library media specialist. An exemplary library media center is described in the following text. Use the accompanying "Library Walk-About Checklist" found in Appendix H to make note of strengths and areas for improvement in the current library media facility.

Lighting and Electrical Outlets

When you walk into the library media center, the overhead and natural lighting creates a bright and cheerful atmosphere. Corners and all instructional and reading areas are also well lighted. Any areas without access to the overhead lighting are illuminated by lamplight. Electrical outlets are plentiful and safe. They are out of students' reach and not overloaded. No cords stretch across open spaces where students will walk. If students have laptops, outlets are available close to or under tables.

Wireless Access

If the students or teachers have laptops, adequate access points are available for uninterrupted reception of wireless signals.

Signage

As you walk through the library, do you know where the fiction books are shelved, where to return or borrow books, and which computers print to which printers? Do you know how much the copies cost? If you don't, then neither do students or teachers. Signs are placed in obvious places and are worded in a positive manner. (For example, replace "NO drinks" with "Water permitted—please recycle!" In other words, instead of displaying signs stating what students cannot do, word them so they promote behaviors you want to see from students and other library patrons.) Bookshelves are marked with the genre, such as fiction or reference, and with the general library classification numbers (usually Dewey Decimal Classification with subject headings) to aid students and teachers in locating materials on the shelves. Computers are marked with their logins, if needed, corresponding printers, and login/passwords for the subscription databases to which the library subscribes.

Bookshelves

On your tour of the library, pass by the bookshelves. Can students reach the highest shelves? Are the shelves no more than three-quarters filled with books? If books are crammed into a shelf, students are not likely to choose those books for pleasure since the books are difficult to remove and reshelve. Do you see books occasionally displayed on shelves at attractive angles or positioned so that they call attention to their titles? Check to see if atlases and dictionaries are easily accessible on stands or separate shelves. If your library has a professional collection, is it where teachers have easy access to it? Freestanding shelves are spaced so that a student with a wheelchair or walker can move through easily and are angled so that the person at the circulation desk can see the aisles.

Seating Area for Pleasure Reading

One area of the library will have comfortable seating, such as sofas or overstuffed chairs or rockers, inviting students and staff to find a book and stay awhile. This section may be close to the fiction books and certainly within arm's reach to the magazines and newspapers. Chairs are placed so that a wheelchair can comfortably fit and move through.

Instructional Area

The main area of seating will accommodate at least one class for instruction. Ideally this space is away from the library book collection so that students from other classes may continue to browse shelves without disturbing the instructional session. Chairs and tables are arranged so students can see the interactive white board or multimedia projector screen. Tables are large enough for students to collaborate in groups and spread out books and writing materials, including laptops when appropriate, and allow adequate space for wheelchairs or walkers. If laptops are used at the school, provide electrical outlets for functioning off AC power.

Story Time and Presentation Area

If your library is in an elementary or primary school, you will have an area for story time and presentations such as puppet plays and storytellers. This area will typically have step-style seating or large cushions and be large enough to accommodate at least one class of children. There will be a chair for the story reader and a display board such as a white board or bulletin board. It may have a puppet theater or small stage. This area may be walled or sectioned off so that it is not easily seen from the main area of the library.

Computer Tables

Your library will have tables that host a bank of computers for students to use for searching the library's online catalog and accessing digital resources. The computers will be placed so the monitors are visible to the librarian and the cables are placed so students will not trip over or unplug them. Adequate electrical outlets will ensure that outlets are not overused. Cords should not stretch across aisles or between tables where students may pass. Chairs are placed so students are not crowding around the monitors. Students have access to paper for jotting notes and book call numbers. Printers are available for students and staff. Computer tables are accessible to students using walkers or wheelchairs.

Circulation Desk

The library has a large desk that is clearly recognizable as the place where students go for help and to check out or check in books. This desk has a computer and printer for the librarian and aide's use as well as a phone and a place for students to return books. There is a comfortable chair for the staff member attending the desk. The area is uncluttered and clearly marked. There are one or more shelves behind the desk to temporarily store materials and books.

Décor

As you are walking through the library, notice the décor. Is it inviting and well maintained? Are book displays, student artwork, plants, posters, or art prints attractively arranged? Is a clock visible from most angles in the room? The library is tidy and uncluttered with trashcans placed in convenient spots. Consider asking parents to professionally frame a selected piece of their child's art and donate it to the school. This is a great way to showcase talent and cover bland library and school walls.

Book Displays

You will see books displayed on tables and shelves and in special display bins. These displays will change frequently and feature such themes as holidays, author birthdays, curriculum topics, new books received in the library, ethnic and cultural recognitions, community celebrations, Children's Book

Week, Teen Read Week, National Library Week, Women's History Month, and Presidents' Day. Bulletin boards will have a library or reading theme and are updated frequently.

Library Media Specialist's Office and Work Space

Your library media specialist's office space has windows with a view of the library, especially the circulation area. The office is uncluttered and will probably have the librarian's diploma or credentials displayed. This space may be adjacent to a work area containing a sink for cleaning equipment, a counter for covering and processing books, and one or more cabinets for storing supplies. The office and the workspace should have locking doors.

Work Space for Students

If yours is a middle or high school library, students and faculty have access to a counter with supplies such as stapler, paper clips, three-hole punch, electric pencil sharpener, tape dispenser, and scissors. Consider having the same items available in the elementary library also.

Storage Room

Materials available in varied formats such as kits, video and audiotapes, DVDs, and math and science manipulatives will be housed in a room with a locking door. The materials are organized by Dewey Decimal Classification (or by subject area) on shelves easily accessed by teachers. Shelves are dust free and neatly arranged.

Open Space

Important in your facilities tour is the amount of open floor space. This encourages library use because it is easy for patrons to move around and get from one place in the library to another. If you have to dodge chairs and tables, step over cables and power cords, and say "excuse me" every few feet to move around students, the library may be too crowded.

Advocacy for the Library Media Program

Libraries today are being devalued, and their purpose is misunderstood in many educational communities. Some even believe that the Internet can replace libraries. Principals, therefore, must be well-informed advocates for library media services, specialists, and centers. Accurate, up-to-date information can assist campus leaders in promoting better library programs as they work and communicate with faculty, central office staff, superintendents, school board members, and the broader community. According to the AASL, advocacy is

- Telling a library story
- Creating conditions that allow others to act on your behalf
- Expanding someone's consciousness

- Evoking or creating memories
- Confirming your identity
- Enhancing awareness, appreciation, and support
- An exercise in creativity and initiative
- An art and a science
- Creating relationships, partnerships, and coalitions
- Respecting other people's views, priorities, and reasons
- A responsibility of leaders
- About potential and the future: the survival of school libraries (American Association of School Librarians, *Advocacy PowerPoint Presentation* slide number 6)

An outdated paradigm of library media centers—a place where library skills were taught out of context and librarians functioned as keepers of books—causes a lack of respect for the prominent place the library media center should hold as a center of learning. Without support and outside-the-school advocates, campus library facilities can become obsolete or fall into disrepair. As noted earlier in this chapter, staffing may also be in peril if district decision makers do not understand the importance of professional library media personnel. An effective advocate is wise about the decision-making environment, knows how to use information and resources well, selects efficient and effective modes of communication, and is keen to the time factors potentially affecting key decisions.

There are a number of ways to draw parents and the broader community into the school's library media center. As the principal, consider the following strategies for helping others learn more about the library media center and its programs:

- Host principal or administrative meetings in the school's library media center and feature the library media specialist as a speaker to briefly address the group
- Submit library media center activities to the local newspapers, school or district newsletters, and to the school Web site
- Showcase library media-related initiatives at regular school board meetings and other community functions
- Feature library media center special events at parent-teacher association meetings or other community gatherings
- Invite the library media specialist to speak about current trends and practices to a parent group

ENABLING DECISIONS AND ACTIONS	PROGRAM AREA	INHIBITING DECISIONS AND ACTIONS
■ Library media program schedule allows for collaborative planning and teaching at point of need in the classroom curriculum ■ Collaboration is a widely shared value at the school and is a standard way of accomplishing instructional goals ■ Classroom teachers understand that the library media specialist has unique expertise and is willing to work side by side with them to plan, teach, and assess	**Collaboration**	■ Library media center is booked with classes that visit the library as part of a set, inflexible rotational schedule ■ Due to accountability system pressures, teachers choose to teach to a test instead of to the *real* curriculum ■ Teachers work in isolation and do not share teaching responsibilities with other professionals on the campus
■ The school employs a full-time library media specialist, or more, if needed on a large campus ■ The school employs a full-time paraprofessional, or more, who assists the library media specialist	**Staffing**	■ Library media center is understaffed for the number of students enrolled in the school ■ School has less than a full-time library media specialist ■ There is no paraprofessional to assist the library media specialist on a regular basis
■ Candidates for a library media specialist's post hold a master's degree of Library and Information Science from an ALA-accredited program ■ Candidates are fully licensed or certified in their state as a library media specialist	**Hiring**	■ Candidates for a library media specialist's post do not hold a master's degree of Library and Information Science from an ALA-accredited program ■ Candidates are not fully licensed or certified as a library media specialist
■ Administrator(s) and librarian engage in annual professional goal setting ■ Administrator(s) make frequent visits to the library media center to observe the librarian at work and to gather and share data, when appropriate ■ Administrators encourage and facilitate peer-supervision activities	**Supervision**	■ Administrators focus only on the annual district mandated evaluation process in which a preobservation or goals-setting conference may or may not be conducted ■ Administrator(s) seldom, if ever, visits the library media center for walkthrough observations during instructional events, activities, or special programs
■ Administrator(s) collaboratively design the master schedule with a variety of campus and instructional needs in mind ■ Administrators help to establish a flexible-access schedule for the library media center ■ Administrators promote the use of the library media center across the curriculum	**Scheduling and Usage**	■ Administrators implement a fixed library schedule or place the library media center into a static weekly rotational schedule with classes such as physical education, art, music, and computer ■ Administrators do not promote or encourage the use of the library media program across all subject areas and grade levels
■ Administrators develop the annual budget with input/requests from divisions, departments, and grade levels including the library media program/library media specialist ■ The budget provides ample funding to replace and renew the library collection on an annual basis	**Budgeting**	■ Administrators establish the annual campus budget without input or requests from faculty or staff ■ Campus programs are allocated a standard annual amount regardless of declared goals, program needs, or special requests ■ Because of inadequate funding, deselected or weeded items may not be replaced

Figure 4.1. Administrative Decisions and Actions Affecting Library Media Practice

- Invite central administrators and school board members to participate in reading events or serve as guest readers in the library

- Sponsor book fairs and special author readings, including featuring student authors

- Make the library media center a focal point in the school by displaying student works of art or other student-generated work there

- Host annual school volunteer appreciation events in the library media center

Essential Concepts for This Chapter

Chapter 4 offers guidance to principals and assistant principals in a variety of administrative areas related to the library media program. Hiring, appraising, budgeting, allocating space, and scheduling are standard administrative tasks. When school leaders understand how their decisions affect the librarian and quality of services she can render, certainly they will strive for best practice actions in each of these administrative arenas. Principals who can talk to others about their library program in an informed manner do much to promote the program and its benefits for all.

Planning for Action and Getting Started

1. Read, learn about, and understand the implications of fixed and flexible scheduling.

2. Ask the librarian about the schedule she follows and how it allows her to collaborate and work with classroom teachers and their curriculum.

3. Review the library's annual budget and discuss with the librarian the cost of replacing and updating weeded or deselected items.

4. Take a walking tour of the library media center and notice how the facility is being used. Talk with the library media specialist about her ideas for reworking the facility or using it more effectively.

5. Assess yourself on the six program areas in the chart "Administrative Decisions and Actions Impacting Library Media Practice" (see Figure 4.1) to determine areas needing improvement.

Works Cited

American Association of School Librarians. *Advocacy PowerPoint Presentation*. Chicago: American Library Association, 2002.

American Association of School Librarians. *Empowering Learners: Guidelines for School Library Media Programs*. Chicago: American Library Association, 2009.

American Association of School Librarians. *Position Statement on Appropriate Staffing for School Library Media Centers*. 14 Aug. 2009. <http://www.ala.org/ala/mgrps/divs/aasl/aaslissues/positionstatements/appropriatestaffing.cfm>.

Gray, Carlyn. "Interview Questions for Hiring a Library Media Specialist." Information sheet. Austin, TX, 2002.

International Federation of Library Associations/UNESCO. *School Library Guidelines*. The Hague, The Netherlands: International Federation of Library Associations, 2002.

Krashen, Stephen D. *The Power of Reading: Insights from the Research*. Englewood, CO: Libraries Unlimited, 1993.

Lance, Keith Curry, Marcia J. Rodney, and Christine Hamilton-Pennell. *How School Librarians Help Kids Achieve Standards: The Second Colorado Study*. San Jose, CA: Hi Willow Research & Publishing, 2000.

Loertscher, David V. *Reinventing Your School's Library in the Age of Technology: A Guide for Principals and Superintendents*. 2nd ed. San Jose, CA: Hi Willow Research & Publishing, 2001.

van Deusen, Jean Donham. "Prerequisites to Flexible Planning." *Emergency Librarian* 23.1 (1995): 16–19.

Additional Resources

Elliott, Donald, Glen Holt, Sterling Hayden, and Leslie Edmonds Holt. *Measuring Your Library's Value: How to Do a Cost-Benefit Analysis for Your Public Library*. Chicago: American Library Association, 2007.

Laughlin, Sara, and Ray Wilson. *The Quality Library: A Guide to Staff-Driven Improvement, Better Efficiency, and Happier Customers*. Chicago: American Library Association, 2008.

Wilson, Patricia Potter, and Josette Anne Lyders. *Leadership for Today's School Library: A Handbook for the Library Media Specialist and the School Principal*. Westport, CT: Greenwood Press, 2001.

Scheduling for the Library Media Program

"AASL Resource Guides for School Library Media Program Development—Flexible Scheduling." 13 Aug. 2009. <http://www.ala.org/aaslTemplate.cfm?Section=resourceguides&Template=/ContentManagement/ContentDisplay.cfm&ContentID=15007>.

Ohlrich, Karen Brown. *Making Flexible Access and Flexible Scheduling Work Today*. Englewood, CO: Libraries Unlimited, 2001.

Position Statement on Flexible Scheduling. American Library Association/American Association of School Librarians. 14 Aug. 2009. <http://www.ala.org/ala/mgrps/divs/aasl/aaslissues/positionstatements/flexiblescheduling.cfm>.

Taylor, Joie. *Information Literacy and the School Library Media Center*. Westport, CT: Libraries Unlimited, 2005.

Budgeting

Budgeting for School Libraries—American Library Association: <http://wikis.ala.org/professionaltips/index.php/Budgeting>.

Budget Planning Guide for School Library Media Specialists: <http://www.bcps.org/offices/lis/office/admin/budgetplanguide.doc>.

Dickinson, Gai K. L. *Empty Pockets and Full Plates: Effective Budget Administration for Library Media Specialists*. Worthington, OH: Linworth Publishing, 2003.

Facilities Planning

Baule, Steven M. *Facilities Planning for School Library Media and Technology Centers, 2nd edition*. Worthington, OH: Linworth Publishing, 2007.

Bryan, Cheryl. *Managing Facilities for Results. Optimizing Space for Services*. Chicago: American Library Association Editions, Public Library Association, 2007.

Erikson, Rolf, and Carolyn Markuson. *Designing a School Library Media Center for the Future, 2nd edition*. Chicago: American Library Association, 2007.

Advocacy

Annette Lamb and Larry Johnson's Web site for educators—Eduscapes: <http://eduscapes.com/sms/advocacy/advocacy.html>.

Doucett, Elisabeth. *Creating Your Library Brand: Communicating Your Relevance and Value to Your Patrons*. Chicago: American Library Association, 2008.

Fisher, Patricia, and Marseille Pride. *Blueprint for Your Library Marketing Plan: A Guide to Help You Survive and Thrive*. Chicago: American Library Association, 2005.

Fisher, Julieta Dias, and Ann Hill. *Tooting Your Own Horn: Web-Based Public Relations for the 21st Century Librarian*. Worthington, OH: Linworth Publishing, 2002.

Schuckett, Sandy. *You Have the Power! Political Advocacy for School Librarians*. Worthington, OH: Linworth Publishing, 2004.

CHAPTER 5

Continuous Improvement and the Library Media Program

> **ⓘ GUIDING QUESTIONS**
>
> What is the relationship of professional development to continuous improvement?
> What are the characteristics of effective professional development?
> What is the principal's role in designing and facilitating adult learning?
> How can the principal support the library media specialist and the library media program in regard to professional development and growth?
> What is action research and how can it affect the library media program and the school?
> How can a self study or program assessment impact the library media program at the campus and district levels?

Introduction

Professional growth and development is essential as educators stay on top of trends, hone instructional strategies, and adjust practices over time for the purpose of increased student performance and continuous school improvement. The librarian's role is twofold in regard to this endeavor—as staff development participant and as staff development leader. This chapter explains this dual role, describing ongoing learning opportunities for the library media specialist as well as the critical role the library media specialist plays in designing and leading learning sessions for teachers, staff, parents, and others in and around the school community. In addition to describing a variety of successful approaches to staff development, including action research, this chapter also addresses how campus administrators support and sustain the professional development agenda for the campus and staff, including pursuing their own professional learning. Last, this portion of the text offers several useful tools for evaluating the effectiveness of the library media program at the campus and district levels.

Characteristics of Effective Professional Development

Each year schools and school districts around the globe spend time, money, and energy on staff development or inservice training sessions. While some professional development sessions are well-planned, aligned with goals and needs of the campus, and represent the best in adult teaching and learning, other staff development activities fall flat. "Staff development has gone by many names—inservice education, professional development, and human resource development. But whatever it was called, it too often was essentially the same thing—educators (usually teachers) sitting relatively passively while an expert exposed them to new ideas or trained them in new practices" (Hayes 6). Poorly planned and orchestrated professional development can cause those involved to cynically view their participation as nothing more than a waste of time.

A growing body of research and professional literature offers guidance in avoiding the pitfalls of ineffective or unsuccessful professional development. Building on a knowledge base and supported by research reports from the 1980s, 1990s, and early 2000s, the common core of characteristics of successful professional development programs include:

1. Involvement of participants in planning, implementing, and evaluating programs

2. A foundation of schoolwide goals but integration of individual and group goals with school goals

3. Long-range planning and development

4. Coherence, marked by the coordination and integration of different professional development activities

5. The incorporation of research on school improvement and instructional improvement

6. Administrative support, including provision of time and other resources during program planning, delivery, and evaluation

7. Adherence to the principles of adult learning

8. Relevant, job-embedded professional development focused on student learning

9. Collegiality and collaboration among teachers and between teachers and administrators

10. Active learning

11. Attention to the research on change

12. Follow-up and support for transfer of learning to the classroom

13. Ongoing assessment and feedback

14. Continuous professional development that becomes part of the school culture (Glickman, Gordon, and Ross-Gordon 336)

Professional development designers have also begun to think about adult learning formats in uniquely different ways, moving away from whole-group, one-topic lectures to an array of approaches. Some contemporary examples include *skill development programs* (workshops and coaching sessions distributed over several months focusing on learning and transferring new skills), *focused institutes* (intensive learning experiences on a single substantive topic), *collegial support teams* (groups of teachers or staff at the same site engaging in inquiry, problem solving, and innovation implementation), *networks* (educators from different schools or locations share, exchange, and discuss information through a variety of electronic and live venues), and *individually planned professional development programs* (an individual sets goals, designs, and carries out a plan of study, and assesses outcomes) (adapted from Glickman, Gordon, and Ross-Gordon 338).

The Principal's Role in Professional Development

Roles and actions of the campus principal in professional development vary greatly based on the philosophy or approach to adult learning practiced at the school. For example, compare the *training approach* with the *professional development model* of learning, described in the following paragraphs.

While a *training model* has its place in new learning for educational professionals, this traditional format is less effective than the more development-oriented philosophies of adult and collaborative learning. Training reflects a "deficit in knowledge" way of thinking—where the "knowledge stands above the teacher" (Sergiovanni 247). In this model the adult learner is considered a consumer of knowledge and the principal is seen as the expert. Individuals who participate in sessions using this method are generally passive and have little opportunity for active application of the topic. The principal or training leader usually delivers the information orally, in a whole-group presentation design.

The *professional development model*, on the other hand, differs from the traditional training approach. Here, the learner stands above the content and constructs meaning through participation.

> In professional development models, the teacher's capacities, needs and interests are paramount...Principals are involved as colleagues. Together, principals and teachers work to develop a common purpose themed to the improvement of teaching and learning. Together, principals and teachers work to build a learning and inquiring community. (Sergiovanni 249)

Many school success stories involve leaders who serve as motivating forces in the learning life of the campus. Such individuals challenge those in the school to consistently learn—a commitment that targets not only the students in the building but the adults as well. These administrators model professional learning and growth in open and highly visible ways.

In a study of schools that transformed themselves into *professional learning communities*, principals were central to increased learning and effective professional development. "These principals continuously scanned the horizon for new information to improve learning...This information was then applied at their schools, where these principals overtly modeled learning and its application" (Hord 23). To increase professional capacities for learning, principals often use strategies such as "developing collegial relationships with staff, focusing staff on student success, making opportunities for teachers to learn, inviting teachers into decision-making and implementation and nurturing new ways of operating" (Hord 23).

One elementary principal's actions illustrate this overt and open commitment to learning. This principal participated alongside teachers in a multiweek summer writing institute where the focus was learning about the components of the writing workshop and the recursive nature of the writing process. During the institute, the principal participated in all activities including writing a reflective work for the group's anthology and crafting an expository piece submitted for professional publication at the close of the three-week session. Not only did she model professional learning for those around her, this principal had a greater understanding of the writing workshop and how it functions in the instructional setting. Consequently, she applied vocabulary and concepts confidently as she talked with teachers, and she provided meaningful information and feedback to staff during supervisory and evaluative visits to the classroom. She offered follow-up and support sessions for teachers as they implemented these new strategies and communicated knowledgeably with colleagues, parents, and the public about the campus's approach to writing. The impact of these actions was felt and seen for years to come as writing as a process became a way of life on the campus. Within several years, virtually all staff members, including the library media specialist, were trained, even though no stipends were paid for attending the summer institute.

Like the principal in this story who learned more about the writing process, campus leaders should commit to knowing more about the library media center and what constitutes an effective program. As noted earlier, most preservice preparation programs for school leaders spend little time, if any at all, focusing on the library and its services. And because administrators influence and shape many facets of the school organization, their actions can effect the operation of the library media program almost as much as the library media specialist can. To learn more, administrators can

- Spend time visiting and talking with the library media specialist
- Read from a variety of professional books, articles, and Web-based resources such as online journals and blogs
- Request assistance or mini-workshops from district administrators or the library media director, if such a position exists in the district
- Become familiar with state and national standards and guidelines
- Occasionally observe or shadow the library media specialist
- Attend specific training with the library media specialist
- Participate in administrator-focused sessions at state and national library conferences

All of these are excellent ways to learn about effective library programs and the role of the library media specialist.

"Job-embedded staff development means that all educators, superintendents, assistant superintendents, curriculum supervisors, principals, school librarians, and teachers, among others, must see themselves as teachers of adults and view the development of others as one of their most important roles" (Hayes 8).

Professional Development for the Library Media Specialist

> For professional development to be meaningful … it must operate on two levels. … individuals should have a variety of learning opportunities to support their pursuit of their own personal and professional career goals. Second … a school and district organization should together define, learn, and implement skills, knowledge, and programs that achieve common goals of the organization. (Glickman, Gordon, and Ross-Gordon 350)

For the library media specialist, who may be one of a kind on her campus, professional learning may take a variety of forms—face-to-face groups, virtual forums, or even independent learning—and should be geared to the specific interests and needs of the individual. While some of the following outlined formats are traditional in nature and quite familiar, others may require additional study and attention to fully understand. Professional development approaches that may benefit the library media specialist include:

Workshops—district, regional, state, national; sessions on topics of needs or interest; typically last one day or longer

Networks—meeting face-to-face or virtually, partnering with public, university, or other school library media specialists in the region or in nearby communities; groups meet to share and discuss common interests and/or needs

Mentoring—meeting regularly with an assigned or chosen individual; sharing thoughts, opinions, and strategies; making and/or taking suggestions

Peer Coaching—working with a colleague of choice; posing questions that stir thought and reflection; providing written and oral feedback at the request of the peer based on an area of interest and/or perceived need

Study Groups and Professional Learning Communities—meeting on a regular basis, either face-to-face or virtually, with a group that shares a common interest; reading/studying material; sharing ideas, thoughts, and opinions

Independent Study and Readings—setting learning goals; generating an action plan with activities for learning such as selecting books, journals, online journals, and databases to read; conducting observations and interviews

Conference Attendance and Presentations—travel funds and release time are required; preconference sessions may be appropriate based on professional goals, needs, and topics offered

Professional Association Memberships—yearly dues required; join local, state, national, international associations; such groups often offer online resources, hard copy and online professional journals and newsletters, electronic forums and training modules, annual conferences or meetings, and webinars

Webinars—learning opportunities delivered live via the Internet, with one or more speakers who typically deliver a short presentation and encourage participation and discussion from the audience

Second Life—the library media specialist attends a seminar in the virtual environment of Second Life, with a notable speaker and other professionals in the virtual audience. Often cosponsored by the American Library Association (ALA) and the International Society for Technology in Education (ISTE)

Electronic Lists—an electronic community of individuals who share a common interest; usually moderated and guided; members join by submitting an e-mail address; typically there is no cost for participation

University Classes—college and university classes on various topics of interest; participants may be able to accrue graduate credit toward a degree or special certificate

Online Classes—classes conducted using an electronic or Web-based format; professor or instructor assigns tasks, poses questions, and generates discussions; students participate in and/or lead discussions; students read from a variety of sources; students complete and submit projects; participants may be able to accrue graduate credit toward a degree or special certificate

Online Training—uses an electronic or Web-based format; typically self-paced modules; may have some limited interaction with a presenter or facilitator

Action Research or Disciplined Inquiry—individual researches an area of interest or need by gathering preliminary data to clarify a research question or topic area, reads the professional literature, constructs an action plan including steps, persons responsible, resources, timelines, and evaluation components, examines outcomes compared to the topic area or research question, makes decisions about next steps or future actions; can be conducted independently or in a collaborative group. (For more detail, see Appendix L, "Action Research as a Tool for Improvement.")

Site Visits—individual or group visits sites in or outside the home district to observe practices, examine facilities, and meet with other educational colleagues on specific topics of interest

---

As already mentioned, it is often appropriate for the library media specialist to participate in professional development alongside classroom colleagues. In the previous example, the library media specialist completed the same summer writing institute as her principal had several years prior. Her participation in this training not only reinforced the campus goal of promoting writing as a process but also gave the library media specialist a vocabulary and level of understanding that put her on par with her classroom counterparts. It was not uncommon for her to assist students by picking up where the classroom instructor left off, integrating the library media center and its functions with classroom assignments by incorporating the writing and information problem-solving processes, helping students to identify and locate materials for reports and essays, and weaving factual information into narratives and short stories. The library media specialist was equally comfortable conducting writing conferences with students and assisting them with prewriting, revision, and editing strategies as they worked toward publication of their writing.

Library Media Specialist as a Professional Developer

As noted earlier in this chapter, the library media specialist is an ideal person to design and lead learning sessions for teachers, staff, parents, and others. Planning and facilitating professional development for others sends a message that the library media specialist is a leader and a teacher of adults as well as students, and, more importantly, has something significant to offer. One of the most compelling ways a principal can support the library media specialist is by encouraging him or her to design and lead sessions both in and outside the school. There are numerous formats and forums for these learning opportunities to take place. They may include:

- Conducting campus workshops
- Facilitating district workshops
- Presenting at faculty meetings
- Working directly with grade levels, academic teams, and departments
- Working with individuals on special topics or areas of interest
- Leading and facilitating study groups
- Mentoring others
- Participating in coaching activities with a peer or colleague
- Working with administrators, supervisors, and central office staff
- Conducting sessions for parents
- Working with groups and individual paraprofessionals
- Assisting and working with other librarians

Experienced library media specialists who have acquired a level of expertise in one or more areas of school library service or curriculum integration and who are accomplished staff developers and presenters, may wish to share knowledge with other professionals in larger forums such as regional, state, national, or international conferences. Such requests should be approved and supported, as these opportunities greatly benefit the individual and increase the prestige of the school, district, and the profession they represent. Likewise, when librarians submit works to journals or publish professional texts, they share critical information and experience while bolstering the reputation of their professional affiliations.

Content of Professional Development Conducted by the Library Media Specialist

As a staff developer and leader of learning, the library media specialist can design, plan, and implement an array of learning opportunities for others. While some sessions will relate to nurturing the close and appropriate relationship of classroom teaching and learning and the library media center, the library media specialist can also lead sessions on topics that may not be readily associated with the library media center. Likewise, she may have specific expertise in one or more content areas, depending on her undergraduate education and previous teaching experiences. Examples of professional development topics may include:

- Integration of information and communications technology (ICT) skills into the content-area curriculum

- Specific strategies related to ICT skills (i.e., note taking, Internet searching, citing sources, Web evaluation, developing research questions, and defining tasks)

- Assessment of ICT skills (designing and using rubrics, scoring guides, and checklists across the process)

- Resources available in the library collection (digital and print copy)

- Reading-writing connection (using literature as a springboard for student writing and reader response)

- Copyright issues (teacher use of copyrighted materials, student use of copyrighted materials, compliance with copyright laws, and fair use guidelines)

- Plagiarism (understanding plagiarism, effective strategies for avoiding plagiarism, creating assignments that help prevent students from committing plagiarism, attribution or citation styles)

- Use of the library media center online catalog and subscription databases (proper use, accessing, and scope)

- Assisting students in selecting appropriate reading materials
- Emerging technologies, including the use of participative tools such as blogs and wikis

It is crucial that library media specialists serve as staff developers for technologies. They are particularly well suited to lead such sessions because:

- They have a healthy attitude toward technology
- They practice effective teaching skills
- They possess a clear understanding of the importance technology plays in information literacy and developing higher-order thinking
- They are experienced collaborators and use technologies successfully
- They have the flexibility to provide on site support
- They have a whole school view
- They understand the ethical and moral issues around the uses of and application for technologies (Johnson 1)

Technology-related sessions facilitated by the library media specialist may include: effectively using the Internet with the classroom curriculum, acceptable use policy and practice, using digital resources, use of technology in the information search process, software applications, and creating multimedia presentations.

As the librarian plans to lead professional development for others, the principal can support these efforts by being actively involved, not only as a workshop participant but also as one who provides resources to make such sessions possible. Needed resources and support may include announcing and promoting the session among teachers and staff, making arrangement for facilities, purchasing materials, supplies, or equipment, providing professional books or articles, funding the duplication of workshop packets, and paying for refreshments for participants. The principal can also help to sustain support over time by encouraging follow-up sessions or providing time for discussion and the extension of ideas during faculty meetings and on designated district and campus professional development days.

Professional Growth for the Paraprofessional

Effective library media specialists and campus administrators recognize the importance of qualified clerical or paraprofessional assistance and the profound impact these individuals can have on the library media program. Because few opportunities for personal and professional development exist for paraprofessionals, other than generic training that is frequently not specific to the library media center's mission or goals, it is the job of the library media specialist to assist in identifying or creating learning opportunities for the paraprofessional. The following list includes local (district and campus-based) possibilities as well as broader-based learning opportunities. As with professional staff, learning and training goals for paraprofessionals should be geared to specific interests, strengths, and challenges. Such topics and situations may include the following:

- Library media specialist can model various on-the-job systems, processes, and procedures for the paraprofessional

- Library media specialist and library media center staff can attend conferences together

- Library media specialist can help to design a list of professional readings and independent study activities for the staff members

- Library media specialist can teach staff the information search process so they may work with others

- Library media specialist can request district training sessions on library automation software or software application such as word processing, spreadsheet, or desktop publishing

- Paraprofessional-specific opportunities may also be available through state and national library associations

Providing Support through Supervision

Another effective model of professional development the administrative team can provide is engaging in supervision activities with the library media specialist. Supervision, which differs from appraisal or evaluation (measuring performance against prescribed benchmarks and standards for the purpose of contract extension or renewal—see chapter 4), can do much to enhance the professional relationship between the principal and librarian.

A conventional supervisory cycle will begin with a face-to-face conversation between the library media specialist and the administrator, during which they will discuss possible instructional goals as well as goals for the library media program. At this meeting the two may also decide on conducting one or more observations so that data can be gathered for the library media specialist. The types of data (e.g., teacher talk versus student talk, levels of questioning, proximity in the instructional setting, degree of collaboration with a teaching partner) should be determined by the library media specialist and related to the goal area or areas she has selected. Tools for data gathering can be constructed collaboratively and will be based on the kinds of information needed. After a visit to the instructional setting, the principal will prepare the information and share it as soon as possible with the librarian (see the following feedback guideline). At a follow-up meeting, the two colleagues can review and analyze information gathered and discuss possible plans of action or next steps. Once one supervisory cycle is complete, another can begin, continuing work on the earlier goals, or establishing a new improvement area.

Another effective supervisory approach can be accomplished through the use of the "Library Media Specialist Instructional Activities Feedback Form" (see Appendix I). This tool directly focuses the administrator's attention on four primary areas of the library media specialist's role: instructional partner, information specialist, literacy programmer, and collection developer. Here the principal or assistant principal can record specific anecdotes and examples of the librarian's work in each of the core areas (observations) while also posing questions and noting issues they are curious about (key questions—please tell me more about these things). In a follow-up session with the librarian, the administrator can share the collected information and use what she has observed and recorded as a springboard for professional dialogue.

Providing useful feedback and information to the library media specialist involves:

- Being descriptive rather than judgmental
- Being specific rather then general
- Concentrating on things that can be changed
- Giving feedback at a time as close to the actual behavior as possible
- Relying as much as possible on information whose accuracy can be reasonably documented (adapted from Sergiovanni 273)

Feedback should flow both ways—from administrator to librarian *and* from librarian to administrator. Using the "Administrator's Library Media Program Feedback Form" (see Appendix J) closes the information loop. In the hands of the library media specialist, this tool provides a forum for communicating about and reinforcing administrative decisions that are allowing the librarian and the library media program to function effectively within the school. Likewise, this form also provides a way to ask for assistance by calling the administrator's attention to challenging circumstances or situations. For example, if the library media specialist wants to make a major shift in the established library schedule to allow more instructional planning and collaboration time, administrative approval or intervention may be required. The librarian can make such a request in the "please consider" section under *the administrator supports my role as an instructional partner* on the "Administrator's Library Media Program Feedback Form." Or, a principal who has provided additional funding in the campus's annual budget for library resources to support the science curriculum can easily be kept informed on the newly acquired items by reading this librarian-provided information ("what's working" in the section *the administrator supports my role as a collection developer*). Although it is customary to think of supervisory information as moving primarily in one direction—from administrators to faculty members—wise school leaders realize they can gain valuable insight about the impact of their administrative actions by engaging in consistent two-way feedback with their campus-based instructional colleagues.

Crafting and Conducting a Program Evaluation or Self Study

Evaluating and examining ourselves from within can help to answer a number of essential questions. How are we performing? Are we meeting the needs of our learners? Are we being good stewards of our allocated resources? Are we making progress toward our declared goals? From a practical standpoint, conducting such an assessment can signal the need for minor program revisions or indicate that we need to completely retool a particular program. A variety of issues can be explored using program evaluation or a self study protocol to help us better understand how to improve the way we do business in our school or district.

A critical step in the self evaluation process is to determine goals or an area of focus for the study, such as comparing program practices to state and/or national standards, gauging the degree of instructional collaboration between teachers and library media specialists, or exploring how the library media collection and program are meeting the needs of an increasingly diverse array of learners. Data collection, analysis, and dialogue over time in a variety of settings will help to reveal assets as well as areas requiring improvement. Once findings are identified, conducting an open session or presentation can help to *make public* the issues that need future attention. "When we assess ourselves from the inside out, we can grapple with the reality of our strengths while honestly owning up to our needs or weaknesses" (McGhee and Jansen 12).

When librarians and campus-level administrators in one public school district decided to engage in a year-long self study, the outcomes were dramatic, resulting in increased library budgets, modified campus schedules allowing for greater teacher and librarian collaboration, and renewed administrative awareness of and respect for the instructional role of library media specialists across the district. (See Appendix K for a set of guide sheets generated for this study on budgeting, scheduling and usage, and staffing.) During the course of the academic year, workshops and planning sessions involving campus principals and assistant principals, librarians, and teachers generated powerful shifts in thinking about the instructional potential of the library media program. When asked what they had learned about the role of the librarian and how it had affected their professional relationship, one administrator responded,

> I had an epiphany ... [the librarian] needs to be part of our leadership team. Our library has undergone a metamorphosis—from a room with books to a vibrant center of learning. She is an incredible asset ... and I now know I can rely on her to enhance instruction and learning on our campus. (McGhee and Jansen 12)

Action Research as a Tool for Improvement

Professional development can have a powerful impact on schools and the professionals and paraprofessional who work in them. While a variety of adult learning formats were introduced in the prior sections, still other frameworks for professional development and reflective inquiry exist and hold great promise for improving programs and practices. One example gaining prominence in the educational field is action research. Stated quite simply, action research is a fancy way of saying let's study what's going on at our school and decide how to make it better (Calhoun).

Action research is a form of inquiry that targets a specific school-based problem or focus area. By applying an action research model or cycle, individuals or collaborative teams can acknowledge concerns, generate improvement strategies, and assess outcomes to determine future actions. "It [action research] provides both the short-term benefits of solving immediate problems and the long-term benefit of teachers' professional development" (Gordon 76). Action research is especially appropriate for schools because it is a method that addresses content-specific situations and can be adapted to meet the unique circumstances of any educational environment.

Steps of a typical action research cycle include:

1. Identify a problem, research question, or an area of focus
2. Collect, analyze, and interpret data
3. Study related literature or possible solutions
4. Craft a plan of action
5. Implement the plan
6. Evaluate outcomes

See Appendix L for more in-depth information on each phase of the action research cycle.

GEARing Up for Success: An Action Improvement Model for Library Media Specialists

As previously indicated, improvement and change occur as individuals and programs grow and develop over time. Using the GEAR (Gather information, Establish goals, Apply strategies, Reflect) method, outlined in the following sections, the library media specialist, with support of the principal or other campus leaders, can develop a habit of inquiry and continuous progress. Yearly application of this model can improve professional practice, help to hone related skills, increase the overall effectiveness of the library media program, and positively affect student performance. Based on the tenets of action research, this four-step model can assist the librarian in achieving the goal of continuous improvement of the library media program. (A variety of guide sheets that support the GEAR method can be found in Appendix M.)

Steps of the GEAR Method

Gather Information: The library media specialist uses data collection methods and sources such as surveys, interviews, observations, student work samples, lesson plans, collection data, circulation data (when appropriate), case studies, archival records, and feedback and comments to assess needs and determine situations. He consults the professional literature and relevant research.

Establish Goals: The librarian designs long- and short-term goals for the program (or for himself) related to the identified areas of need based on the literature and effective library media practice.

Apply Strategies: The library media specialist facilitates the implementation of strategies for improvement.

Reflect: The library media specialist compares outcomes or results to long- and short-term goals and makes decisions about next steps or additional or new goal areas.

Successfully Applying the GEAR Method

Included here is an example of using the GEAR method in the area of collaboration between the library media specialist and fifth-grade teachers.

Scenario: The library media specialist notes that all of the teams except fifth grade are collaborating with him to integrate information and technology skills into their subject-area curriculum. With the support of the principal, he uses the GEAR method so that fifth-grade students can reap the benefits of integrated content and skills.

Gather Data: The library media specialist keeps records of all times fifth-grade students request assistance for research. He keeps anecdotal observations of how fifth-grade students independently locate and use print and electronic resources and the struggles, challenges, and successes they experience.

Establish Goals: The library media specialist writes these goals: Attend fifth-grade team meetings on a regular basis or as often as possible. Begin establishing rapport by offering to collect and organize materials and online resources for units under development. Follow through. By third or fourth meeting, collaborate with teachers to integrate information and technology skills into their assignments. Follow through.

Apply Strategies: The library media specialist uses records and anecdotal observations to convince teachers to collaborate. He reviews with them the steps of the information search model that the students used in fourth grade and suggests that the students will be more efficient in locating and more effective in using information if they use these steps. He designs motivating and meaningful instruction for students to practice using the library's print and online collection of resources. He schedules and delivers instruction to students. He follows through.

Reflect: The library media specialist considers how efficiently and effectively students located and used information by assessing their results. He evaluates their interaction with each step of the information search process. He assesses the attitudes of the fifth-grade teachers in the collaboration process and in their students' performance during each step of the process.

Essential Concepts for This Chapter

Professional growth and development is crucial to the health and well-being of any educational professional. Motivating activities closely aligned with the needs of the individual can greatly improve practice over time. The librarian shoulders a dual role in professional learning—as participant *and* leader. This chapter highlights these two facets of professional development. Besides describing successful formats for adult learning, this chapter also notes how campus administrators support and sustain the professional development agenda while also pursuing their own professional learning. Action research is a form of professional development that promotes continuous improvement for individuals or collaborative groups. Engaging in program evaluation or self studies are powerful and effective ways to gauge the success of campus or district initiatives. The GEAR method is an improvement model for library media specialists based on the action research cycle. Using this improvement process can positively affect the librarian and his work across the school and the curriculum.

Planning for Action and Getting Started

1. Review the elements of successful professional development and effective adult learning.

2. Schedule a supervisory cycle with the library media specialist and learn more about his goals for the program.

3. Encourage the library media specialist to design and facilitate professional development sessions at faculty meetings and other whole-school gatherings.

4. Promote the library specialist as a professional developer by encouraging him to submit proposals for state and national conferences and meetings.

5. Introduce the faculty to the concepts of program evaluation, self study, or action research as continuous improvement tools.

6. Assist the library media specialist with the GEAR Method and promote this action cycle as a path to improved practice.

Works Cited

Calhoun, Emily. *How to Use Action Research in the Self-Renewing School*. Alexandria, VA: ASCD, 1994.

Glickman, Carl D., Stephen P. Gordon, and Jovita Ross-Gordon. *Supervision and Instructional Leadership*. 8th ed. Boston: Allyn and Bacon, 2010.

Gordon, Stephen P. *Professional Development for School Improvement: Empowering Learning Communities*. Boston: Allyn and Bacon, 2004.

Hayes, Karen. "School Librarians as Staff Developers." *The Book Report* 19.4 (2001): 6–8.

Hord, Shirley, ed. *Learning Together Leading Together: Changing Schools through Professional Learning Communities*. New York: Teachers College Press, 2004.

Johnson, Doug. "Becoming Indispensable." *School Library Journal* 49.2 (2003): 3.

McGhee, Marla W., and Barbara A. Jansen. "A District-Wide School Library Self Study: A Story of Improving from Within." *Library Media Connection* 27.2 (2008): 12–13.

Sergiovanni, Thomas J. *The Principalship: A Reflective Practice Perspective*. Boston: Allyn and Bacon, 2001.

Additional Resources

Professional Development and Instructional Supervision

Bishop, Kay, and Sue Janczak. *A Staff Development Guide to Workshops for Technology and Information Literacy: Ready to Present!* Columbus, OH: Linworth Publishing, 2004.

Daresh, John. *Leading and Supervising Instruction*. Thousand Oaks, CA: Corwin, 2006.

Farmer, Lesley S. J. *Your School Library—Check It Out!* Westport, CT: Libraries Unlimited, 2009.

Harlan, Mary Ann. *Personal Learning Networks: Professional Development for the Isolated School Librarian*. Westport, CT: Libraries Unlimited, 2009.

Lindstrom, Phyllis H., and Marsha Speck. *The Principal as Professional Development Leader Building Capacity for Improving Student Achievement*. Thousand Oaks, CA: Corwin Press, 2004.

National Staff Development Council. 14 Aug. 2009. <http://www.nsdc.org/>.

Tallerico, Marilyn. *Supporting and Sustaining Teachers' Professional Development: A Principal's Guide*. Thousand Oaks, CA: Corwin Press, 2005.

Action Research, School and Classroom-Based Research, and Inquiry

Farmer, Lesley S. J. *How to Conduct Action Research: A Guide for Library Media Specialists*. Chicago: American Library Association, 2003.

Glanz, Jeffery. *Action Research: An Educational Leader's Guide to School Improvement*. Norwood, MA: Christopher-Gordon, 2003.

Howard, Jody, and Su Eckhardt. *Action Research: A Guide for Library Media Specialists*. Columbus, OH: Linworth, 2005.

Hubbard, Ruth, and Brenda Power. *The Art of Classroom Inquiry*. Portsmouth, NH: Heinemann, 2003.

Moore, Rita. *Classroom Research for Teachers: A Practical Guide*. Norwood, MA: Christopher-Gordon, 2004.

Sagor, Richard. *The Action Research Guidebook*. Thousand Oaks, CA: Corwin, 2005.

Stringer, Ernie. *Action Research in Education*. Columbus, OH: Pearson Education, 2004.

Sykes, Judith A. *Action Research: A Practical Guide for Transforming Your School Library*. Westport, CT: Libraries Unlimited, 2002.

Administrator Self Assessments for Important Chapter Concepts

Administrator Self Assessments for Important Chapter Concepts

I KNOW A LOT ABOUT...	CONCEPTS IN CHAPTER 1	I WANT TO KNOW MORE ABOUT...
❏ Notes:	There are research findings showing evidence that a strong library media program increases student achievement.	❏ Notes:
❏	There is a link between integrated information and communications technology skills and the tested curriculum.	❏
❏	The American Association of School Librarians published a set of national guidelines for school library media programs.	❏
❏	The state has a set of standards for school library media programs and our school should meet or exceed the minimum standards.	❏

Figure A.1. *Principal's Guide to a Powerful Library Media Program* Administrator Self Assessment: Chapter 1

I KNOW A LOT ABOUT...	CONCEPTS IN CHAPTER 2	I WANT TO KNOW MORE ABOUT...
❏ Notes:	The national standards published by the American Association of School Librarians and the International Society for Technology in Education address the needs of the 21st-century learner.	❏ Notes:
❏	An information search process can help students stay organized when finding information for their curricular needs.	❏
❏	The school library media specialist collaborates with teachers to integrate the search process and information and communications technology skills into the content-area curriculum.	❏
❏	The school library media program promotes reading, writing, and visual literacy across the curriculum.	❏
❏	The school library media program champions intellectual freedom and equal access to ideas and information, while addressing ethical issues such as copyright and plagiarism.	❏

Figure A.2. *Principal's Guide to a Powerful Library Media Program* Administrator Self Assessment: Chapter 2

Administrator Self Assessments for Important Chapter Concepts

I KNOW A LOT ABOUT...	CONCEPTS IN CHAPTER 3	I WANT TO KNOW MORE ABOUT...
❏ Notes:	In her role of information partner, the school library media specialist (LMS) collaborates with teachers, teaches information and communications technology (ICT) skills at point of need in the content-area curriculum, and usually assesses ICT skills.	❏ Notes:
❏	As an information specialist, the LMS uses technology tools and resources to engage students with ideas and information, introduces effective new technologies to faculty and students, promotes the ethical use of ideas and information, and works with the school's professional community to design and develop curriculum that integrates ICT skills and an information search process.	❏
❏	As a literacy programmer, the LMS engages students in a variety of activities and programs that promote reading for pleasure.	❏
❏	In her role as collection developer, the LMS develops a culturally responsive collection and collaborates with teachers and students to select materials that meet all needs and interests.	❏
❏	As a program administrator, the LMS has dozens of additional responsibilities that may or may not directly involve instruction but that keep the library media program and its resources accessible to students and the greater school community.	❏

Figure A.3. *Principal's Guide to a Powerful Library Media Program* Administrator Self Assessment: Chapter 3

Administrator Self Assessments for Important Chapter Concepts

I KNOW A LOT ABOUT...	CONCEPTS IN CHAPTER 4	I WANT TO KNOW MORE ABOUT...
❏ Notes:	The school has met the minimum requirements for staffing the library media center based on the state and national guidelines.	❏ Notes:
❏	I engage in annual goal setting with the library media specialist as I would with any other member of the instructional faculty.	❏
❏	The library media specialist is an active participant in the campus-level budget planning process, and the program is adequately funded to further the school's curricular mission.	❏
❏	The library media program's schedule permits time for the librarian to collaborate with teachers and teach at point of need in the curriculum. It also allows for maximum use of its facilities.	❏
❏	As a library media program advocate, I showcase the library media program and communicate with others about its critical instructional role.	❏

Figure A.4. *Principal's Guide to a Powerful Library Media Program* Administrator Self Assessment: Chapter 4

Administrator Self Assessments for Important Chapter Concepts

I KNOW A LOT ABOUT...	CONCEPTS IN CHAPTER 5	I WANT TO KNOW MORE ABOUT...
❏ Notes:	Professional development is a key component of continuous growth for all faculty, staff, and administrators and works best when the effective attributes of adult learning are taken into account and practiced.	❏ Notes:
❏	Professional development for and by the library media specialist not only enhances the knowledge base of faculty and staff but also promotes sustained professional learning for and about the library media program.	❏
❏	Supervision is an extension of professional development and differs significantly from the annual appraisal or evaluation process. It is accomplished through consistent and meaningful observation and two-way communication/feedback between the library media specialist and myself.	❏
❏	Our library can evaluate its effectiveness to the school's instructional program by engaging in a self study.	❏
❏	Action research is used to improve professional practice, and the GEAR method is a process that helps the library media specialist increase her effectiveness in one or more areas of responsibility.	❏

Figure A.5. *Principal's Guide to a Powerful Library Media Program* Administrator Self Assessment: Chapter 5

Evaluating Collaborative Units of Instruction

The following is an example of the types of questions that library media specialists and teachers may ask as they collaborate in designing a unit of instruction. You may find that some of the following items do not meet the needs of particular objectives or standards; however, by checking as many as possible, you will ensure that you are designing an effective and engaging experience for students. Included here are the basic steps that all information search processes use. Add the label for each step of the process you are using. You will most likely need to modify the criteria to meet the steps of the information search process you are using.

First, are you using the appropriate terminology of each step of the information search process with the students as you take them through the process?

Do your students know that they are using a *process* to find and use information when they are engaging in the activities and that this process can be used any time they need information for a task or problem?

Developing the Task

Is the task engaging? Will students want to study the content?

Is the task developmentally appropriate?

What about the task is higher level?

Do students have an opportunity to construct what they want to know, or think they need to know about the topic before you tell them specific information to locate?

Is the task closely tied to the state's or school's curriculum standards?

Does it reflect the higher-level thinking of the standards?

Choosing and Locating Resources

Are the resources:

____ developmentally appropriate?

____ readily available and easy to access?

____ accessible to students who may not read on grade level? Who is able to help them?

____ accurate, authoritative, and relevant?

Are students using a variety of resources?

Are students using a combination of electronic and print resources as appropriate?

Which online sources (subscription-based and free Web) will your class use to complete the project? Are students developmentally capable of selecting relevant Web sites, or are you choosing these for the class?

Which primary source materials are students using?

Are you teaching or reviewing how to locate the resources?

How are students accessing information within the materials? How do you know they will succeed at this?

Acquiring Information

How do you know students will be able to access the section of the resource in which the information appears?

Are you teaching or reviewing how to take notes and cite sources? Are students developmentally capable of taking notes? If not, what help do they need in recording information? Who needs to be available to help?

What type of note-taking organizer are students using? Do they need instruction in using this organizer?

How are students evaluating sites off the free Web for accuracy and authority, or are you giving them the sites they are to use?

Are you evaluating sites off the free Web that the students will use?

Presenting Results

How are students organizing information from a variety of sources?

How are students showing evidence of higher-level thinking in the creation of the final product?

Are students learning transferable skills (technology, composition, production, performance, presentation) in the creation of their final product?

How are students giving credit to the sources they used?

Student Self Evaluation

Do students have an informal written self evaluation of their efforts?

Do students have a set of predetermined criteria to judge their efforts in a more formal way (such as a rubric, scoring guide, or checklist)? This may be the same instrument you will use to give them their grade(s). This instrument will usually be given during the task development phase of the assignment.

Assessment of Student Performance

How will you assess student? Rubric, scoring guide, checklist?

Who is creating the assessment instrument?

Will the library media specialist and other members of the team help with the assessment? If not, how will the results of the assessment be shared with all members of the collaborative team?

After Students Complete Unit of Instruction:

How successful was the level of student engagement?

How effectively were the learning objectives met?

How successful was your collaboration with the school librarian or classroom teacher in the completion of this project?

What changes need to occur next time for maximum student practice and mastery of content and skills?

Will you present this unit again?

APPENDIX C

Providing Access to Materials through the Library's Catalog (Cataloging and Circulation)

Cataloging provides physical and intellectual access to all library materials. Classification is one component of cataloging that categorizes materials into subjects through a controlled vocabulary. Standard circulation procedures allow the student or teacher to leave the library with the desired book, DVD, or other material. This combined practice standardizes access to the collection so users have the same access in any school, public, or academic library they use. If the library's physical collection (and increasingly, digital collections are being cataloged for easier access) is not cataloged in a central location in the district, or if the library media specialist cannot purchase the individual records to add to her online catalog, then she must adhere to a strict standard when creating original catalog records. The multistep process to providing access to materials in the physical (and online) collection takes an inordinate amount of time.

Most school libraries use the Dewey Decimal Classification System and Library of Congress or *Sears* subject headings. The library media specialist should have specialized training in cataloging and classification. Knowledge of the cataloging and classification systems, as well as the software and services used to create and organize the MARC—MAchine Readable Cataloging—records for each title, is necessary and not easily learned. MARC records are the electronic version of the information found on a card in a traditional card catalog, but they contain much more data than is viewable to the user. A library media specialist does not always need to create original MARC records. All book suppliers and many individual publishing companies will provide professionally created MARC records with book and audiovisual orders. Occasionally these records are provided free of charge, but usually an additional cost is added for each item in the order. Book jobbers and other companies have fee-based subscription services that allow the campus or district cataloger to access and download records directly into the library's online public access catalog, or OPAC. The Library of Congress allows free access to its records, and many state and school library consortiums provide their members with free access to records. These records will need to be edited for usability on the library's catalog. Copy cataloging is an acceptable practice; however, one must be cautious of the varying quality of records. If a district has several schools, library automation software companies offer a union catalog, allowing the schools to combine their records into one large database, searchable by all. This expedites interlibrary loans and allows for the sharing of MARC records.

If the library media specialist has a strong working knowledge of cataloging and classification, then she can train the paraprofessional to modify and add local information (such as call numbers) to existing records. While paraprofessionals may be capable of learning how to create MARC records, they should not be required to do so since it is a very specialized process and must maintain an industry standard. It is not within the scope of the paraprofessional's duties, as maintaining a quality catalog should be the responsibility of the professional.

Many schools have an OPAC that is available on the library's computers or those in classrooms if the school has a local area network (LAN). These electronic catalogs can be searched in many ways including by subject, author, title, series, as well as keyword, which allows for the entire record to be scanned, providing more points of access and a successful search. Students no longer have to thumb through drawers of catalog cards, limiting their search capabilities and increasing the amount of time locating a single title. If the OPAC has a Web interface and the school district maintains a Web server, students can search the collection from school or home, provided that they have a computer with an Internet connection. Individual titles can also be linked to quality Internet sources of the same subject. Some library automation software companies are now providing the Web access to schools so they no longer have to maintain the Web server. If your school library still maintains a card catalog, strongly consider upgrading to at least an OPAC, and preferably a Web version also.

It is important to maintain quality and use the standard tools, which include Anglo American Cataloging Rules (which will soon be replaced by the new standard, Resource Description and Access), and the Dewey Decimal Classification and Relative Index (most school libraries use the abridged version, but this is not necessary), the Library of Congress or *Sears* Subject Headings, and MARC format. The library media specialist should have these materials available and know how to use them if records are not available from other sources.

Circulation of Library Materials

The circulation of materials requires that a barcode be assigned to each item and that the barcode number attached to the local information in the MARC record. Each teacher, student, and staff member will have a patron barcode assigned to him or her. The item barcode and the patron barcode are both scanned when an item is brought to the circulation desk for checkout. Various methods are used to indicate the date the item is due back in the library. When the item is returned, the barcode is scanned with a specialized device that prompts the circulation software to recognize the item as returned. There are various methods for attaching the date that the item is due back in the library. If the item is overdue, the library staff will send a note or e-mail to the teacher or student. Often a letter sent via U.S. mail or a phone call is required to get a student to return a delinquent item. Once trained, a paraprofessional, parent, or student volunteer can perform most circulation tasks. However, only the library media specialist or the paraprofessional should handle overdue notices, due to privacy issues and respect to the student or teacher.

Library Media Specialist Interview Questions

This guide will help as you interview a candidate for the position of library media specialist. Provide one for each member of the interview committee.

Library Media Specialist Interview Questions

QUESTION	STRENGTHS OF RESPONSE	AREA OF CONCERN
Briefly describe your view of the role of the library media specialist as a member of a professional learning community.		
What kinds of collaborations are appropriate for librarians and teachers?		
Define the term "flexible scheduling" as it applies to the library and tell how you would convince a teacher who did not want to do flexible scheduling to embrace it.		
A teacher wants to schedule her class to visit the library at the same time once a week for a library lesson and book exchange. How will you convince her to allow her students to exchange books several times per week and plan with you for instruction as needed in her curriculum?		
How do you stay current on emerging technologies, especially as they apply to the library media program?		
How do you see emerging technologies supporting instruction, and what role does the library media specialist play in integrating these tools?		
How do you decide what information and communications technology skills to teach to students and when they should be taught in the curriculum?		
Describe the role of the library paraprofessional.		
How would you publicize a special library activity?		
Tell us about a recent professional or staff development activity you found beneficial.		
How would you use parent/community volunteers and student assistance to support your campus library media program?		
What experience have you had in building a school library budget?		
Explain why it is important for a school district to have an instructional materials/book selection policy.		
Define a culturally responsive collection. How would you go about developing one for our school?		
A teacher requests that you duplicate a DVD from the local video store. What would you do?		
How will you educate teachers and students about ethical issues such as copyright and intellectual property?		
If we were able to talk to the students you have worked with, what would they tell us about you?		
As a librarian, to what professional organizations do you belong?		

Figure D.1. Library Media Specialist Interview Questions

Paraprofessional
Interview Questions

This guide will help as you interview a candidate for the position of library paraprofessional. Provide one for each member of the interview committee.

Paraprofessional Interview Questions

QUESTION	STRENGTHS OF RESPONSE	AREA OF CONCERN
Please describe your organization skills and strengths.		
What experience do you have working with children?		
Suppose you are assisting several students who need to check out their library books when a teacher sends a student to the library media center with a request for assistance. What would you do?		
Tell us about your experiences working with others in a collaborative setting.		
How would you approach and work with a group of noisy students in the library?		
A student in your school has a book out that is now six weeks overdue and wants to check out another book. How would you handle this situation?		
You are helping a student with the online catalog and the phone keeps ringing. What would you do?		
Describe your proficiency with technology tools.		

Figure E.1. Paraprofessional Interview Questions

Library Media Program Budget Proposal Worksheet

Use this worksheet to share with the budget committee the requests and rationale for funding the library media program. See Chapter 4 for further details.

For school year: _____

Library Media Program Budget Proposal Worksheet

BUDGET CATEGORY AND CODE	PRESENT YEAR'S AMOUNT	REQUESTED AMOUNT FOR NEXT SCHOOL YEAR	RATIONALE
General supplies Code:	$_____	$_____	
Library books and professional collection Code:	$_____	$_____	
Periodicals Code:	$_____	$_____	
Audio-visual equipment Code:	$_____	$_____	
Audio-visual software (CD-ROM, DVD, etc.): Code:	$_____	$_____	
Online subscription databases Code:	$_____	$_____	
Bookbinding Code:	$_____	$_____	
Equipment repairs and cleaning Code:	$_____	$_____	
Support agreements for circulation/cataloging software Code:	$_____	$_____	
Conference registrations and travel Code:	$_____	$_____	
Professional organization membership fees Code:	$_____	$_____	
Promotional and special reading events Code:	$_____	$_____	
Other Code:	$_____	$_____	
Other Code:	$_____	$_____	
Other Code:	$_____	$_____	
Comments:			

Figure F.1. Library Media Program Budget Proposal Worksheet

Library Media Program Budget Worksheet

Use this worksheet to keep track of expenditures and plan for the following year. See Chapter 4 for further details.

For school year: _____

Library Media Program Budget Worksheet

BUDGET CATEGORY AND CODE	ALLOCATION	SPENT OR ENCUMBERED	NOTES FOR NEXT YEAR'S BUDGET REQUEST
General supplies Code:	$_____	$_____	
Library books and professional collection Code:	$_____	$_____	
Periodicals Code:	$_____	$_____	
Audio-visual equipment Code:	$_____	$_____	
Audio-visual software (audio, video tapes, CD-ROM, DVD, etc.): Code:	$_____	$_____	
Online subscription reference databases Code:	$_____	$_____	
Bookbinding Code:	$_____	$_____	
Equipment repairs and cleaning Code:	$_____	$_____	
Support agreements for circulation/cataloging software Code:	$_____	$_____	
Conference registrations and travel Code:	$_____	$_____	
Professional organization membership fees Code:	$_____	$_____	
Promotional and special reading events Code:	$_____	$_____	
Other Code:	$_____	$_____	
Other Code:	$_____	$_____	
Other Code:	$_____	$_____	
Comments:			

Figure G.1. Library Media Program Budget Worksheet

Library Walk-About Checklist

Use this guide as you and the library media specialist walk through the library to assess its appeal and functionality for the school community. All areas should be accessible for wheelchairs. The explanations for each section are described in detail in Chapter 4.

Library Walk-About Checklist

AREA IN LIBRARY MEDIA CENTER	STRENGTHS OR WEAKNESSES	SUGGESTIONS FOR IMPROVEMENT
Lighting and electrical outlets ❏ Bright and cheerful ❏ Outlets safe and plentiful ❏ Cords are out of the path		
Signage ❏ Placed in obvious areas ❏ Positive wording ❏ Bookshelves marked logically ❏ Computers and printers identified with proper information		
Bookshelves ❏ Accessible to all students ❏ Shelves contain some empty space—books are not crammed ❏ Atlases and dictionaries accessible ❏ Placed so that wheelchairs can move through		
Seating for pleasure reading ❏ Comfortable seats available ❏ Adequate lighting ❏ Wheelchairs can move through		
Instructional area ❏ Seating accommodations for at least an entire class ❏ Chairs and tables arranged so students can see overhead display ❏ Large tables for collaborative groups ❏ Adequate room for wheelchairs ❏ Electrical outlets for laptops		
Story time and presentation area ❏ Step-style seating or cushions ❏ Walled-off or separate from instructional area		

(continued)

Library Walk-About Checklist

AREA IN LIBRARY MEDIA CENTER	STRENGTHS OR WEAKNESSES	SUGGESTIONS FOR IMPROVEMENT
Computer tables ❑ Monitors visible ❑ Cable placement secure ❑ Electrical outlets are within fire code ❑ Chair placement not overcrowded ❑ Paper available for note taking ❑ Printers available ❑ Wheelchair accessible		
Circulation desk ❑ Large and clearly recognizable ❑ Computer and printer for library staff's use ❑ Phone for library staff ❑ Book return area ❑ Comfortable chair ❑ Uncluttered and clearly marked ❑ Shelving for temporary storage		
Décor ❑ Inviting and well-maintained ❑ Book displays, etc., arranged in appealing design ❑ Clock visible to students ❑ Tidy and uncluttered		
Book displays ❑ Books attractively displayed on tables, tops of shelves or bins ❑ Displays change frequently		
Office and work space ❑ Windows have view of library ❑ Adequate shelving ❑ Adjacent to work space with counter ❑ Supply cabinets ❑ Locking doors		
Audio-visual storage room ❑ Organized by Dewey Decimal System or other system ❑ Shelves accessible ❑ Dust-free and neatly arranged		

Figure H.1. Library Walk-About Checklist

Library Media Specialist Instructional Activities Feedback Form

Library Media Specialist Instructional Activities Feedback Form

Instructional Partner (e.g., collaborate—plan, teach, and assess—with teachers to integrate information and communications technology skills; design and develop curriculum)
Observations:

Key Questions (please tell me more about these things)

Information Specialist (e.g., instruct students to use technology tools and resources to engage with ideas and information, introduce new technologies, promote ethical use of information)

Observations:

Key Questions (please tell me more about these things)

Literacy Programmer (e.g., create reading incentive programs, host authors/storytellers, promote booklists, develops knowledge of genre/authors, conduct book talks, encourage reluctant readers)

Observations:

Key Questions (please tell me more about these things)

Collection Developer (e.g., collaborates with teachers to select resources, reads reviews, and selects quality materials; develops culturally responsive collection)

Observations:

Key Questions (please tell me more about these things)

Administrator's Library Media Program Feedback Form

Administrator's Library Media Program Feedback Form

The administrator supports my role as an instructional partner
(ex: library media specialist collaborates—plans, teaches, and
assesses—with teachers to integrate information and communications
technology skills).

What's working:

Please consider ...

The administrator supports my role as an information specialist
(ex: library media specialist instructs students to use technology tools
and resources to engage with ideas and information, introduces new
technologies, promotes ethical use of information).

What's working:

Please consider ...

The administrator supports my role as a literacy programmer
(ex: library media specialist creates reading incentive programs, hosts
authors/storytellers, promotes booklists, develops knowledge of genre/
authors, conducts book talks, encourages reluctant readers).

What's working:

Please consider ...

The administrator supports my role as a collection developer
(e.g., library media specialist collaborates with teachers to select
resources, reads reviews, and selects quality materials; develops
culturally responsive collection).

What's working:

Please consider ...

Guide Sheets for Library Self Study—Budgeting, Scheduling and Usage, and Staffing

Guide Sheets for Library Self Study—Budgeting

SCHOOL: _____
BUDGET PLANNERS: _____
What's working now?
1.
2.
3.
4.
5.
What do we want to do differently or what do we want to think about changing (consider enrollment projections, collection development related to curriculum focus areas, professional conferences/travel, etc.)?
1.
2.
3.
4.
5.
Steps needed or ideas for accomplishing our budgeting goals (district funding, campus funds, categorical aid, grants, foundation dollars, special fundraising initiatives, parent or support group funding, etc.):
1.
2.
3.
4.
5.

Figure K.1. Library Media Program Budget Planning

Guide Sheets for Library Self Study—Scheduling and Usage

SCHOOL: _____
SCHEDULING AND USAGE PLANNERS: _____
What's working now?
1.
2.
3.
4.
5.
What do we want to do differently or what do we want to consider changing?
1.
2.
3.
4.
5.
Steps needed or ideas for accomplishing our scheduling goals:
1.
2.
3.
4.
5.

Figure K.2. Library Media Program Scheduling and Library Usage

Guide Sheets for Library Self Study—Staffing

SCHOOL: _____
STAFFING PLANNERS: _____
What's working now?
1.
2.
3.
4.
5.
What do we want to do differently or what do we want to consider changing?
1.
2.
3.
4.
5.
Steps needed or ideas for accomplishing our staffing goals (include here budget considerations, space allocations, responsibilities, training and professional development, etc.):
1.
2.
3.
4.
5.

Figure K.3. Library Media Program Staffing Ideas

APPENDIX L

Action Research as a Tool for Improvement

Following is in-depth information on each phase of the action research cycle.

Identify a problem, research question, or an area of focus

The action researcher begins the inquiry process by determining whether there is sufficient evidence to indicate a specific problem or area of need. In this initial phase it is critical to make certain that the problem is accurately identified and verified with data to guard against implementing a solution rather than zeroing in on a real problem. This may require that a needs assessment be conducted by the researcher or research team using tools or information such as questionnaires, interviews, focus groups, observations, or on-site archival quantitative and qualitative data (i.e., school performance records, standardized achievement data, student success rates, attendance information, open-ended satisfaction surveys).

Collect, analyze, and interpret data

As mentioned in the first phase of the action research process, focusing on the *real* issue is key to making a difference with action research. That is why having multiple sources of information that point to the same problem is considered best research practice. In collecting and managing data, the researcher must also be mindful of ethical issues related to confidentiality, informed consent, and parental notification. Analysis and interpretation of the data requires the researcher to note trends, patterns, and themes as they begin to make meaning of their findings.

Study of the related literature

Unfortunately, this is a rare practice in schools. Reading and understanding empirical research, theoretical works, or even opinion pieces requires time and energy that busy school leaders do not often have. Yet this is one of the most vital activities in an effective improvement process. Studying articles, books, lectures, and electronic or Web resources, as well as attending conferences or engaging in professional conversations with other educators, can help schools avoid the pitfalls of ineffective programs. These resources can point action researchers in the positive direction of best or most promising practices related to their research area or topic.

Craft a plan of action

The action plan is the heart of the action research process. In this step, researchers use all information gathered to this point (data, problem area or focus, results of the literature review) to develop a comprehensive plan that will actively focus on the identified area of concern or need. In addition to objectives, tasks, or programs selected for implementation, the planner should also address related components like timelines, required resources, and persons involved or responsible for each activity or action step.

Implement the plan and evaluate outcomes

After implementing the action plan, the researcher addresses questions such as: Did it work? How is it working? Have we made a difference? How do we know? In this step of the cycle, the researcher may return to many of the data sources examined early in the process, collecting follow-up data to gauge progress or outcomes. This is also the time to consider reporting on or sharing results with stakeholders such as students, parents, colleagues, administrators, central office, board, or the professional community. This is the phase in which next steps and future endeavors are determined.

Works Cited

Calhoun, Emily. *How to Use Action Research in the Self-Renewing School*. Alexandria, VA: ASCD, 1994.

Gordon, Stephen P. *Professional Development for School Improvement: Empowering Learning Communities*. Boston: Allyn and Bacon, 2004.

GEAR Worksheets for Concepts in Chapters 2 and 3, Including Blank Worksheet

GEAR Worksheet for Concepts in Chapter 2

Library Media Specialist: _____

Date: _____ Date Reviewed: _____

TOPIC OR THEME	GATHER DATA	ESTABLISH GOALS	APPLY STRATEGIES	REFLECT
Choose an information search model				
Collaborate with teachers				
Integrate information and communication technology skills into curriculum				
Ethical use of information— intellectual freedom, copy- right, and plagiarism				

Figure M.1. GEAR Method Planning Guide for Concepts in Chapter 2

GEAR Worksheet for Concepts in Chapter 3

Library Media Specialist: _____

Date: _____ Date Reviewed: _____

TOPIC OR THEME	GATHER DATA	ESTABLISH GOALS	APPLY STRATEGIES	REFLECT
Instructional partner				
Information specialist				
Literacy programmer				
Collection developer				

Figure M.2. GEAR Method Planning Guide for Concepts in Chapter 3

GEAR Worksheet for Concepts

Library Media Specialist: _____

Date: _____ Date Reviewed: _____

TOPIC OR THEME	GATHER DATA	ESTABLISH GOALS	APPLY STRATEGIES	REFLECT

Figure M.3. GEAR Method Planning Guide Worksheet

Index

curriculum *(continued)*
  high school art history, 29
  intermediate grade social studies and
    language arts, 26, 55
  primary grade science and social studies, 24
  intermediate grade science, 24
  middle school grade math, 27
  high school social studies and language
    arts, 28
  high school environmental science and
    English composition, 30

D

Daresh, John, 102
Darrow, Robert, 36
databases
  online subscription, 51, 57, 76
Davidson, Susanna, 60
department heads, 5
deselection. *See* "collection:weeding"
Dewey Decimal Classification System, 76, 111
Diamont-Cohen, Betsy, 60
Dickinson, Gail K., 60, 62, 83
differentiate instruction, 19, 47
Discovery Streaming, 31
diversity, 33
Doucett, Elisabeth, 83
Drew, Bernard A., 61
DVDs, 32, 44

E

ebooks. *See* books: electronic
Eckhardt, Su, 102
Edminister, R. William, 38
educational service centers, regional, 41
effective schools
  Effective Schools Correlates, 3
  principal's support of literacy learning, 5
  role of the principal, 3
EGS Research and Consulting, 13
  *Texas School Libraries: Standards, Resources,
    Services, and Students' Performance*, 13
Eisenberg, Michael B., 36
Eisenberg, Michael B. and Berkowitz, Robert E.,
    36
electronic resources, 25, 31, 33, 100, 109, 134
  electronic databases, 33, 51, 57
  electronic lists, 91
elementary schools, 47, 48, 72, 75
Empowering Learners: Guidelines for School
    Library Media Programs, 12, 36, 59

encyclopedia, 19, 24, 44, 70
English language arts, 8, 16, 17
EQAO [Education Quality and Accountability
    Office assessment], 7
equal access, 33
equipment
  audio-visual
    purchasing, 69
Erikson, Rolf, 83
ethical issues, 15, 16, 32, 38, 42, 65, 75,
    115, 133
  censorship, 32, 111
  copyright, 67, 68, 75, 82, 66, 104, 115
  intellectual freedom, 32, 65, 66, 94, 96, 99
    Library Bill of Rights, 32, 65
  plagiarism, 104
ethnic celebrations, 48
evaluation, 80, 87
  difference from supervision, 95
events, budgeting for, 70

F

facilities, 63, 75, 79
  access, 77
  arrangement, 75
  audio-visual storage, 78
  book displays, 49, 77, 124
  bookshelves, 76
  circulation desk, 54, 77, 78
  computers, 78
  décor, 77
  decoration and useability, 75
  electrical outlets, 75
  instructional area, 78
  lighting, 75
  office and work space, 78
  open floor space, 78
  planning, 62, 83
  story time and presentation area, 77
  student artwork, 77
  Walk-about Worksheet, 75
  walking tour, 75, 81
Farmer, Lesley, 60, 102
feedback, 4, 5, 87, 89, 90, 96, 97, 99, 107,
    125, 127. *See also* "supervision"
fiction, 32, 45, 49, 51, 52
Fink, Elaine, 13
first Colorado study, 6
Fisher, Julieta Dias, 83
Fisher, Patricia, 83
Foss, Kathleen, 38

Franklin, Patricia, 62
funding, 34. *See* budgeting

G

GEAR method, 99, 100, 135–138
  applying strategies, 99–100
  establishing goals, 99–100
  gathering information, 100
  reflection, 100
GEARing Up for Success, 99
gift items, 41
Gillespie, John T., 61
Glanz, Jeffery, 102
Glickman, Carl D., xxiii, 13, 22, 37, 101
goals
  campus, 69, 86, 97
  learning, 42, 95
  paraprofessional, 95
  professional, 87, 90, 96, 99
  program, 95
  short and long term, 79, 99, 100
Google Docs, 21
Google Earth, 46
Gordon, Stephen P., 3, 13, 87, 90, 98, 101,
    104, 134
Gray, Carlyn, 66, 82
Grimes, Sharon, 38
guest authors, 48
guest storytellers, 48
Gupton, Sandra Lee, 13

H

Halsall, Jane, 38
Hamilton-Pennell, Christine, 13, 64
Harada, Violet, 37, 59, 60
Harker, Christa, 37, 59
Harlan, Mary Ann, 102
Harvey, Carl A., 37
Hatfield, John T., 61
Hayden, Glen, 82
Hayes, Karen, 101
health, 27
high schools, xxiv, 16, 21, 71
higher-level thinking, 18, 109, 110
Hill, Ann, 83
Hinton, KaaVonia, 60
Hoerr, Thomas, 13
Hoffman, Gretchen McCord, 38
holidays, 32, 77
Holt, Glen, 82
Holt, Leslie Edmonds, 82

Hopkins, Janet, 38
Hord, Shirley, 102
Howard, Jody, 102
Hubbard, Benjamin J., 61
Hubbard, Ruth, 102
Hughes-Hassell, Sandra, 37

I

IFLA/UNESCO, 69
iGoogle®, 42
Impact of School Library Media Centers on
    Academic Achievement, the, 6
Increasing Academic Achievement Through
    the Library Media Center: A Guide for
    Teachers, 17
Individual Evaluation Profiles, 19
information and technology skills, 16, 36, 41,
    42, 44, 45, 49, 50, 57, 66, 72, 73, 78,
    80, 81, 86, 89, 100, 121, 125, 126
  integrated instruction, 7
  integration with content skills, 7, 68
  point of need integration, 43, 45, 85
information literacy, 1, 5, 6, 36, 42, 82, 94, 102
*Information Literacy: Essential Skills for the
    Information Age*, 36, 72
information problem-solving. *See* "information
    search process"
information process skills
  integration into literacy programs, 48
information search process, 15, 16, 18, 20,
    21, 22, 23, 24, 45, 47, 56, 94, 100,
    104, 108
  as framework for collaboration and
    teaching, 18
  definition, 16
  Eisenberg and Berkowitz Big6 Skills Approach,
    18, 36, 72
  integrating instruction, 15, 71
  Stripling Inquiry Process, 37
  when to use, 16
instruction
  bibliographic, 45
  content meaning, 18, 47
  contextual, 16, 79
  developmentally appropriate, 24, 52
  direct, 21, 49
  individualized, 19
  instructional materials, 34
  instructional spaces, 75
  integrating content and process skills, 18, 45
  methods, 11